Awakening After Life

Awakening After Life

A Firsthand Guide through Death into the Purpose of Life

Rene Jorgensen

Visit www.booksurge.com to order additional copies.

Awakening After Life

Table of Contents

Acknowledgments

First, I would like to acknowledge the first natives of the land of North America from where I am speaking. Then, I wish to thank my wife for her unconditional love and support that has made it possible for me to write this book. Valerie, the beautiful light that you shine on me and the world is a true manifestation of the Light that I am writing about. Thank you.

I also wish to thank the many teachers and helpers on my path. I thank you all for letting the light in you shine on me so that I am now able to pass it on. Then, a special thank to the International Association of Near-Death Studies (IANDS) and all its members for their brave and important research into the phenomena of the near-death experience.

For help with editing my 'foreign language,' I wish to thank Karen at First Editing and I especially want to thank my publisher Book Surge Publishing for making it possible for me to share this book with the world. Also, many thanks to Evelyn for her help and support in guiding the light of my experience into this dimension.

Introduction

Dear Reader,

You are about to embark on an incredible journey into the true nature of reality. This book is the story of my meeting with a clear bright light of infinite love beyond human comprehension that I had in March of 2000. In this profound spiritual experience, a very deep near-death experience, the ultimate nature of reality—the source of God—was revealed to me. This meeting radically changed my life, and so, I am writing this to you in hope that my story and my insight will inspire you.

With this wish in mind, I have chosen the title *Awakening After Life* to emphasize the importance of us awakening before we die. It was my experience that the true purpose of life is first revealed to us when we die, and therefore, I wanted to share the message of my experience—now. Life has profound meaning beyond our understanding, and not to acknowledge the essence of life is to take away the purpose of living. Realness is discovered in the deepness of life, and the deeper we enter it then the more real it becomes.

Thereby, this book is a journey of investigation into the heart of life based on my personal experience. Rather than only telling my story, I have chosen to investigate the nature of it through the knowledge that we already have available. In this way, I will take you with me on my personal path to discovery of my own experience, and in doing so I will reveal what I have learned from the Light.

The book is split into two parts. The first part, which is entitled *The Afterlife*, has five chapters and examines the afterlife. The first chapter begins by telling the story of my personal awakening from my near-death experience. I only tell my story directly in the first chapter, but you will find that my personal experience is always there indirectly underneath. In this manner, we are on a journey of discovery together—as I examine the near-death experience, religion, philosophy, and science, I will reveal the deeper layers of my insight.

This leads me to my intention, which is the second part called *Awakening*. This part has six chapters and I have written it to inspire the awakening to the Light. Building on the first part, I integrate my own road to awakening as I walk towards the Light in this dimension. This road will lead to an in-depth understanding of how to live in the Light here and now, and finally how to enter it when your life is over. Thus, you will learn what has been called "the ultimate lessons of the Light"—keys that opens the door to heaven in life and hereafter.

Now, this is no small feat for me to set and in my sincere efforts to communicate this message from the Light, I ask you to bear in mind that the true nature of my experience is beyond comprehension. If I should forget, please remind yourself of the paradox between experience and language, and the line between certainty and uncertainty. Also, if my perspective does not fit with your view and understanding, I ask you kindly only to take from what I offer that which inspires you on the path to your truth.

I also wish to say that this is a work in progress as I will probably investigate this mystery all my life. In this process, I invite you as my reader to contribute with insights and suggestions that can help to further the topic. You are more than welcome to contact me through my website at www.AwakeningAfterLife.com.

Welcome Home!

Rene Jorgensen

"It was love.
It requires no explanation,
just as the universe needs none
as it travels through endless time."

- Paulo Coelho

To Valerie

PART I

THE AFTERLIFE

Chapter One

An Awakening

I begin this first chapter with the story of my own awakening because this experience lays the foundation for the rest of this book. I have chosen to share my experience openly in the hope that my story will be a testimony of the essence of life, and serve as a source of inspiration for all my readers. I also hope this openness will reveal the source of my conviction so that you as my reader can independently make up your own mind about my interpretations.

What happened to me is truly beyond human comprehension. But even though there is no language to explain the mystery of my experience, its profoundly indescribable message has spoken so clearly to me that I feel obligated to share it. Many of us too often forget the true nature of life beneath the world we live in, and therefore, my goal is to share the truth my experience taught—that the true nature of life is love.

My awakening happened at the age of twenty-seven. Up until this point in my life, I had spent practically all of my life completely centered on myself. My mother and father spilt up when I was one year old, and as an only child I was brought up in a very materialistic way. My mother, carrying her own load from childhood, had her share of bad luck with love, and by the time I was beginning school, she had given up on the idea. So, what was passed on to me was a shattered idea of love, and instead I was given money and material things to make up for this lack.

This upbringing made me very selfish, even though by nature I was warm inside. I saw the world through my eyes only, and I did not have much compassion for anyone else but myself. I was also an atheist. I had been inside a church maybe five times in my life, when an occasion had forced me to go. I had no religious belief at all, and when people used to talk about God to me, I would say, "If God is real, then where is the proof?"

I only believed in things that I could see or touch, and surely not in anything that was bigger than me. The world in which I lived had convinced me that happiness was only to be found in material things, and so, I pursued a career in business to ensure the continuation of this kind of happiness. After working in sales, I was now completing business school, focusing on a career in marketing.

As the time to begin this new career drew closer, I became aware of a resistance, an emptiness, inside me. Something seemed to be missing, but I could not put my finger on what that was. This emptiness had been with me since my teenage years, and during some periods in my life, I would lose myself in alcohol and drug abuse to try and fill this empty hole. Fueled by anger, I also found myself getting involved in fights without really knowing why. I had clearly felt the effects of this uneasy emptiness again and again, but I did not know what it meant.

Now, at this point in my life, the emptiness seemed to push me to ask questions about life. I felt that there had to be more to life than what I saw and felt and touched in the world I knew. As ridiculous as this seemed to me at the time, I wanted to break free and look for answers.

Then, completely unexpectedly, my father died. He suffered a stroke and died that same day. I received the news the next day, on my birthday, as the first call early in the morning.

I was deeply shaken up, and all of a sudden I felt confused about everything. I was left with the responsibility of arranging the funeral alone, and as I endured this singular and solitary pain, I was forced to look inside in places that I had never looked before. For the first time, I felt life being present at a deeper level. I was in touch with a new part of myself that made me ask the question: "What is the purpose of life?"

Since I could not get the answer to this question from the world that I was living in, I decided to go elsewhere to look for it. This was my calling to let go of what was holding me back. I backed out of a job offer, and one month later, backpack in hand, I was on an airplane to Thailand.

Several months into my journey, I met a girl from Japan. We became travel partners and decided to go to India together. India was a magical place unlike anywhere I had ever been before. It seemed to be frozen in time, and something old of the world was still alive there. My Japanese travel partner was also a new experience for me. Even though my practical reasoning made me keep my distance, and I did not allow myself to fall in love with her, there was something very different about her. I found myself continually observing her. While I did so, she would also observe me and soon she began to reflect my mirror image back to me.

Many times, she would look right through me, and there would be nowhere to hide. She would point to a part of my heart that was closed, and I would be forced to look at myself. Little by little, she would open me up. It was as if she was always a step ahead of me, and that somehow she knew more about the universe than I did. This would sometimes scare me and I would feel naked to the bone.

Time passed, and soon our travel would come to an end. Being rational, I had already prepared a goodbye speech. I planned to thank her for our time together, and suggest that we could stay connected by e-mail. But this was not her idea of a goodbye, and what was to happen next was unimaginably far from anything I could have expected.

On this day we had taken the drug LSD while we were relaxing on the beach getting ready to watch the sunset. We were talking about something, when she suddenly paused, looked right into me and said, "I feel we have been family in a past life."

I was totally unprepared for this, and my mind stalled. I had never believed in reincarnation—remember, I didn't even believe in God—but in the moment she said it, I truly felt it. It all fit together. Our meeting, what had happened to me, the way I was opened up, and the universe around us, all came together in this infinite moment. A deep feeling of recognition overflowed inside me, and my heart felt that it was true.

But this feeling was too much for my mind. Her approach was too strong for me, and she was taking me where I was not prepared to go. I had nowhere to run and I felt like a little kid who was being exposed in lying. So, at the same time my mind was saying, "No, this cannot be possible." Reincarnation—past life connection—I could simply not contain all this.

The moment opened up to infinity, and what it revealed was beyond my comprehension. I was now in unfamiliar waters with a feeling of groundlessness that I had never experienced before. The split between my mind and my heart created a conflict within me. This conflict was between the old me, and the new me that was ready to be born. A power from within me revealed itself and fought the old part in me. For the first time, my ego was fighting to stay alive in an endless uncharted ocean. My ego was begging for mercy, but there was no mercy to be found. My feeling of groundlessness expanded and became so powerful that it threw me out of my body.

I was suddenly no longer observing what was happening from inside my body. I now found myself outside my body in the air above where we were sitting. My awareness was moved to a place outside my body, maybe ten or fifteen yards in the air. From here, I could look down and observe both her and my body sitting on the beach. I was looking down from a bird's eye view as a third person and it were as if I were a point of space of infinite awareness.

The sensation of being pulled from my body was overwhelmingly powerful. I felt a deep explosion, like a volcanic eruption, pull my body apart and dissolve the essence of what I once knew as myself. I was suddenly naked, exposed to everything in the entire universe, but at the same time I was bathed in the transparent light of something so powerful, so indescribable, all words fade and disappear.

It was love. I melted together with a feeling of love a hundred or maybe a thousand times stronger than anything I have ever felt in this dimension: "This is truth—this is what it is!" In that moment I knew the universe, "This is who I am—this is all there is!"

What I experienced was my true nature as absolute and unbound consciousness. In this state there was nothing that I did not know—all knowledge was there. It was as if I had come home to my self—home to the ultimate nature of reality—home to love. It was *all* love. As I consumed all the love gathered from all the stars in the universe, I broke out in awe, "Wow! I did not know!"

My heart was now thrown into a black hole by the consequence of this realization. It is all love—but I did not know. Through this revelation, I now also realized what was not love. The separation between what I had known in my life to be true and this unimaginable profound revelation created a pain within me. In the chasm of this separation arose a great torment; I had lived my whole life against my own true nature—against love. Out of this separation a deep regret was born and I now started to see my life in review.

In my review I saw all the people that I had hurt throughout my time on Earth. It was like a movie being played out right in front of my eyes, and it showed me all the pain and suffering that I had caused others. First, I saw my mother crying and broken as I shouted at her in anger. I saw how the pain cut deep into her, and I saw myself doing the cutting.

Then I saw an ex-girlfriend. I had cheated on her. Now her whole world was shattered, and her heart was broken by my selfish action. In fulfilling my own desires, I had not cared about her feelings. All the trust and hope that she had placed in me, I had turned to dust and disillusionment. As I felt her agony, I felt disgusted by my actions.

Then I saw an episode in school which I had long forgotten. A small girl was standing against the wall in the schoolyard and I was teasing her. She was lost in her tears and wanted to disappear forever. I was calling her names, telling her she was worth nothing. I felt how the shame I caused that day would expand throughout her life and consume her happiness. She would be less outgoing and less able to love herself as an adult. I felt the full effects this would have on her family and the loved ones around her.

I was horrified. An overpowering feeling of torment crushed my heart on behalf of all the people I had hurt in my life. Having realized the true nature of existence to be infinite love and now seeing myself causing all this pain was devastating. The essence and purpose of life was love, but I had gone against love and therefore my own true nature. It was as if I had been doing all this to myself—by hurting others I had hurt myself. We are all connected—we are all one. From the deepest part of my heart, I cried, "How could I do anything other than love?"

Then I saw the world. I saw all the pain and suffering in it. I saw all the poor people, and all the people living in misery. I saw all the conflict and all the wars in our world. This was far too much for me to bear. My heart could not contain all the world's grief. In an extremely intense sensation, I felt my heart literally tear in two, and the pain was so strong I could not bear it. We live in a world with so much agony, all against the nature of love. How could we accept all this? How could we live the way we do, not seeing the sorrow, not feeling the pain?

At that moment, I knew that I had to do something to change this. I could no longer be an innocent bystander, a mere witness to this unending misery. I had to do something to help all these tormented souls.

Then the feeling of pain changed back into the feeling of love again. I again recognized this almost uncontainable powerful sensation of love as my essence. This was who I am—this was all that there is. With this feeling in me, I now looked to the future in front of me. It was a clear bright light, and I knew that this was the direction in which I would go. I saw myself loving people around me, having compassion for others, and devoting my life to helping the world. At the end of my life, I saw myself entering this light to return to where I came from, and I knew that this was where I would go when my life was over.

After this look into the future, I now came back into my body. In front of me, my friend was sitting looking at me, her lips moving. Everything seemed to be slowing down, and after a brief moment, my hearing came back. I had no idea exactly how long time I was outside my body. It felt like a lifetime, or at least several minutes. It was certainly long enough to open up a window that contained my whole life. When the slowdown stopped, and I could hear her speak again, she was finishing what she had just said before I left my body. So, to her I had not been away for more than a second or two.

But I could not talk to her. My mind was totally blown away, and I felt empty inside my head. I had no grounding at all in the reality of her conversation. It was as if the whole universe had just opened itself to me, and the entire universe was now in my head. In one moment, my consciousness had expanded to the size of the universe and there was no room for me. I was unable to think, and felt totally disconnected from my old self, as if my soul had just been born as a newborn child within me.

The expansion of my consciousness lasted for days. I saw colors more brightly, and there was energy around every object I looked at. I experienced life in a deeper and more profound way—it was all magic.

That same night I had a powerful dream that connected me to my experience. The dream was so real that I felt fully awake inside it. I dreamed that my body dissolved into energy and the energy from my body mixed with the universe above. This release of my energy was an immensely powerful sensation, just as my experience earlier had been when I felt my body. To totally release my energy, I had to let go of my physical self. But this scared me, because I was worried about what would happen to my body. This thinking about my body made me return to it; then the dream was finished.

This dream came back to me for many nights over the following weeks. Every time, it was the same problem: I could not let go of my body. On the last night of the dream, I finally found the strength to let go. All my energy now flowed into the air and my energy merged with the universe above. My energy was totally released from my body, and it flowed into the universe. I was no longer my body or a separate energy; the universe and I were one.

From above, being totally freed of my body, I could now look down to see what had happened to it. When I looked down, I saw my body curled up in a fetal position: it was waiting to be born again. I realized that I had been holding on to my body by worrying about it. And now, being free of it, I felt that I had the choice to return to it or not.

From this dream, I understood the nature of existence, and the cycle of life. My true nature was the flow of energy in eternal existence. This flow is one big cycle of energy. We come from the energy, and we return to there. I also understood how it was possible to be freed from this cycle. What had made me return to my body was the fear of letting go of the physical world.

Coming Back

A few days after my experience, my friend and I parted. She had to go her way and I had to go mine. I am sure she knew something had happened to me, but I am not sure that she fully understood what it was. At this time I did not even know what it was! I did try to contact her again but did not have much luck, so the end of our trip became the end of our connection.

After I returned from my journey, my head felt split in two. I wanted to understand what had happened to me, but with no previous knowledge of such an experience, I was unable to comprehend it. Ironically, I had always asked for the proof of God's existence, and when I finally received it, it was too big for me to handle. The answer was far bigger than the question. The powerful revelation I had experienced could simply not be contained within the constructs of my mind. All my life I had been living in one world, the physical world, denying the possibility that any other world existed; but now I had to admit the existence of another world because I had been there. And this other world was far more real than the reality I knew.

This split between the two realities created confusion in my mind. Which one was the real one? In addition, it worried me that my life-altering experience occurred under the influence of drugs. What if everything I had experienced was a gigantic illusion? These questions made me fear that I had lost my mind, and trying to tell other people what had happened merely made things worse. People rejected the possibility that there was more to life than meets the eye, and some would say I just had a 'good trip.'

Having tried drugs many times before, I knew that this experience was very different. It presented an alternate reality so real that I was convinced it was not a hallucination caused by the drugs. My experience with drugs had always been either a positive or negative inflation of reality, and afterwards I would definitely know it was not real. But this experience was beyond all that—it was more than real. I knew that what had happened was something out of this world.

Finally, I looked up a therapist with whom I could talk about my experience. For little over a year, I went through psychotherapy to help me understand what had happened to me. My therapist explained that I had had a "dramatic ego death experience," in which I had been confronted by a spiritual insight I was not prepared to understand. She explained that, according to Carl Jung, I had had an experience of the Self that lies beyond the personal ego.

My experience had of course been fertilized by the drugs, but she did not put too much emphasis on this issue since she believed that it was the ego death experience that had caused me to leave my body. As I have become more articulate in explaining my experience, I have come to put less and less emphasis on the drug usage and more on the psychological dissolution as the triggering event. One thing that guided me in this direction is the typical reaction of young people, who say, "Wow, I want to try that too!"

I am well aware that skirting the drug issue may open me up to accusations of withholding information. But in this day and age, I do not wish to advocate the use of drugs, and also I do not think that drugs are necessary to perceive the true nature of reality. In my case, my ego was so inflated and my heart was so hardened because I was fundamentally unable to love. This is not true for everyone. So I hope people will listen to the message of my experience rather than turning me off because of the circumstances in which it was conceived.

My therapist turned out to be a very important step in bringing me back to myself, or I should say to my new self. It was a big help for me at the time, and I was happy that my therapist, using Jung's theories, could help integrate my experience. I soon regained my inner balance and grounding in this world again.

Coming back to this world I found myself changed in a big way. I was no longer afraid of dying and, therefore, I was no longer afraid of life. This meant that I now found the strength within myself to love more and show compassion. This came out in all my connections with people from my family to strangers on the street. It was as if the profound experience of the light had stayed with me and was now shining from within. Instead of feeling separate from other people, as I did before, I now felt connected with everyone through my experience of the light. I felt that the light was part of me and that by connecting to it I also would connect to the light in others.

One important way this came out was through my forgiveness list. Still acutely aware of the people I had hurt throughout my life, I made a list of every one of them that I could remember, and then began to contact them one by one. This was a truly great experience of healing. I learned that as I asked for forgiveness from the people that I had hurt, I not only lifted a weight off my own shoulders but also off theirs. By asking forgiveness I made everything right again, and the healing power of this was amazing.

At the same time I also became very curious about where I had been and what I had seen. Therefore, I began a spiritual walk in search of answers. A few months later, I was on a meditation retreat in France when I had another powerful experience. Through meditation I was able to once again go beyond the constructs of the mind, and enter the same state I had experienced in India. This time I did not leave my body and it was a less dramatic experience, as I vividly felt the peaceful unification with nature and things around me. I recognized that I was at one with everything, and I knew that this oneness was my true nature.

Even though I did not leave my body, I had returned to the same place. This confirmation of my experience was an important step for me, and I soon became confident in going beyond the conceptual mind. For me, this was the real proof that I had not lost my mind in India but instead had had a powerful awakening, and now I began to study and learn more about the nature of mind.

Through the study of Buddhism, I came across the words of Soygal Rinpoche: "Death is a mirror in which the entire meaning of life is reflected."[1] After reading these words, there was no longer any doubt in my mind what had happened to me: I had looked into the mirror of death, and the meaning of life had been reflected back to me.

In my spiritual search, I found confirmation everywhere I looked. Whatever the religion or tradition, essentially they were all pointing in the same direction and the direction they were pointing towards was the light. This gave me confidence in the universality of the ultimate reality of the light and reassured me that what I had experienced was real.

Then I came across the research done on the near-death experience. To my surprise (and relief) I found that these stories were the most detailed, step-by-step descriptions of my own experience. When I read about these experiences—meeting the light, feelings of love and joy, and the life-review, then I knew that this was exactly what had happened to me. All of these thousands of accounts of the same experience—*my* experience—convinced me that this was not of my own creation. Of all the places that I looked, I could not find a more accurate testimony to my experience, and this was now an experience that was subject to research and scientific investigation.

At first I had only described my experience as an out-of-body experience, because even though I felt I had been *in* death, I had not literally been near to physical death. But then I learned that the near-death experience can also be caused by the drug that I had taken and through the experience of fear or a powerful spiritual inspiration. If the mind is overwhelmed by fear and thinks it is near death, the mind can trigger a "fear-death" experience. This sounded exactly like my experience of ego death. I also learned that the term "near-death experience" is describing an experience that is too broad to only include experiences that occur near to physical death.

Through this understanding the near-death experience now gave me a new in-depth language based on scientific method to describe my experience. I was also happy to read about other people who had had the same experience. I learned that the life-changes I had sought and made are common to many people who have had near-death experiences. The fear of death disappears, and people find more room for love and compassion. Without the fear of death, the light inspires a trust in the goodness of life that gives more courage to love.

This made me understand the power and importance of the near-death experience. I realized that the profound reality beyond our human dimensions has an essential and powerful message for the evolution of humankind. Therefore, I began to study the near-death experience in the context of philosophy and religion.

Chapter Two

The Near-Death Experience

The term "Near-Death Experience" (NDE) was coined in 1975, when Dr. Raymond Moody published his research in the book *Life After Life*. Moody's interest began after he had come across two similar accounts by two independent individuals who had nearly died. Both told amazing stories of passing into a bright clear light. Connecting the experience of the light to being near death, Moody then focused his research on people who had been pronounced clinically dead but had come back to the world of the living.

Today, over thirty years later, the research into this phenomenon has shown that this experience is not unique to people who have been close to death. The International Association of Near-Death Studies writes that, "Although being close to death is a fairly reliable 'trigger,' identical experiences happen under very different circumstances, even to people who are in no way close to physical death."[1]

In a survey, the International Association of Near-Death Studies found that 37 percent of people who had a "near-death" experience did so in a setting that could not be called life-threatening. Even so, these experiences were as real and life-changing as those experienced by people who were near to death.[2] Both trauma and illness also produces the experience and religious mystics immersed in deep prayer or meditation may also experience the same phenomenon, as well as people under the influence of drugs like LSD.

From all of this it would seem evident that there are many different doors that open up to the same experience, no matter what we chose to label this phenomenon. It does seem very possible that it is a universal experience that has always been experienced by humans. Among the old Greeks, Plato's story of the soldier Er who returns from the dead shows a remarkable resemblance to contemporary accounts. And among the ancient Shamanistic cultures we find journeys into the spirit world, which also seem similar to the NDE.

For this reason, while in my experience I was not literally near to death, there were enough points of convergence that we would seem to be talking about the same phenomenon. While I often call my personal episode a mystical or even Kundalini experience, these are not terms that are part of our present toolbox of languages and concepts. Therefore, I find the near-death experience is the best way to describe what happened to me. When I read the stories of other people who have had near-death experiences, I find that these experiences are identical to my own. This label is what brings me closest to my experience.

At the same time, I am fascinated by the scientific studies currently being done on the NDE. There are thousands of reports of near-death experiences from all over the world and it is estimated that over 65 studies have been done involving more than 2,500 people who have had near-death experiences. Even though scholarly articles on the phenomenon go back all the way to 1889, the last thirty years has seen an explosion in written articles on the subject.

This means that I can not only put my own experience to the test, but also investigate the nature of it. In other words, my experience—which has probably been around throughout all of history—has received new attention through the term near-death experience and the use of modern scientific investigation. So, to follow the paradigm of our time I choose to align my experience with this phenomenon.

Choosing this path also meant that I would have to submit my own experience to inquiry and reflection. The first thing that I checked, of course, was the drug issue. I clearly felt that my experience was much more than a 'good trip,' but I needed to be sure. From my late teens till my mid-twenties, I had had enough exposure to drugs, including LSD, to know that this experience was something altogether different. What happened to me was clearly something that cannot be compared with any drug-induced state that I have ever been in before.

Other people have been asked this same question as well. In one survey, people with near-death experiences were asked whether following the experience they had ever had any other event in their lives, including states caused by medications or substances, which reproduced any part of the experience. The clear majority of 81 percent answered "no," indicating that this experience is clearly something unique.[3]

This is also my experience. I know what a dream is, and I know what an illusion or hallucination is too. But this experience was very different. Near-death researcher, P. M. H. Atwater, explains that:

Hallucinations, no matter how they're caused (and that includes oxygen deprivation, drugs, centrifugal spinning, and blood loss), are either distorted or representative—an invention of the mind. They focus on what isn't or what could be, while deflating or inflating the ego. Their intensity fades with time or leads to increasing periods of confusion. Conversely, near-death states, regardless of type, are clear and coherent—a recentering of the mind.[4]

What makes an NDE different is that it takes the experiencer into another dimension, and yes, when I say another dimension I really mean another world. Like many others, I left my body and entered into this other realm from where I was looking down on myself *from the outside*. This is the element of the experience that makes it different than any dream, illusion or hallucination.

Another researcher, Dr. Melvin Morse tells us the same:

NDEs are not like any hallucinations we know of, nor are they akin to drug-induced hallucinations, schizophrenia, transient psychosis, psychotic breaks, anaesthetic reactions, or dreams. The near-death experience is a logical and orderly event...People who have them know what is happening to them. Unlike people who have hallucinations or episodes of mental illness, NDErs have a feeling of being in control of the situation and do not feel detached from their being.[5]

One could still suspect that the near-death experiences reported by people who have actually been near to physical death would be different that those experienced under the influence of drugs. Here the confirming research that these are the same types of experiences has been done by Stanislav Grof, who is known for his research into psychedelic experiences using LSD therapy.

In his psychedelic therapy with dying cancer patients at the Maryland Psychiatric Research Centre, he gained interesting evidence of the similarity between near-death experiences and experiences caused by psychedelic drugs. Some of his cancer patients who had first had psychedelic experiences induced by drugs later had 'real' near-death experiences that were not drug induced. These patients said that the two experiences were very similar.[6]

Grof concludes that, "The effects of LSD are not unique but reflect a universal potential," from where the experiences share similarities with near-death experiences.[7] For some reason, this drug opens up to the same phenomenon as what is experienced in the NDE.

Melvin Morse also confirmed this when he applied the *Near Death Validity Scale* by Kenneth Ring to the published reports of Grof. According to this scale, the accounts of people in psychedelic therapy scored as moderate or deep near-death experiences. And therefore, also Morse concludes that LSD produces experiences that are identical with the NDE.

To confirm this, I personally took the *Bruce Greyson NDE Scale* to see if my experience would qualify as a near-death experience. This near-death experience scale has a rating from 0 to 32, where 7 and above characterizes the experience as a near-death experience, and 15 is the average score for NDEs. Not only did my experience qualify as a near-death experience, but my score also showed that I had had a very deep NDE. My result, explained by Dr. Bruce Greyson: "Your experience was rather 'deep' on the NDE scale, with a total score of 27 out of 32...What that means is that your score was among the top 4 % of NDEs in terms of 'depth.'"[8]

The Evidence from a New World

The near-death experience is an anomaly that defies the scientific logic of our modern world, and therefore it is often met by skepticism. This is understandable to me, since before my experience, as an atheist, I would also have been very skeptical of the NDE. If I had known about it then, I would certainly have rejected the reality of the experience on the grounds of lack of solid proof.

This paradox makes me think of Columbus before he sailed out into the ocean. Back then the end of the ocean represented the end of the world for most people, who still believed that the earth was flat. But by sailing beyond the horizon and into the end of the world, Columbus proved that the earth was in fact round. In the case of the near-death experience, if we keep an open mind I am confident that it is possible to see beyond the horizon, where I truly believe that, like Columbus, we too have found something at the end of the world.

A *U.S. News & World Report's* poll in 1997 estimated that up to 15 million Americans might have had a near-death experience.[9] The most famous recent case is the near-death experience of ABC anchor, Bob Woodruff, who was almost killed by a roadside bomb in Iraq. He tells us about his experience that,

I don't remember hearing it. I remember that I—I went out for a minute. I saw my body floating below me and [a] kind of whiteness. I don't have much more information than that, whether it was heaven or something. I still don't know.[10]

Most scientific studies are done retrospectively many times years after the experience, but recent prospective studies have shown the experience to be scientifically predictable. In 2001, the first prospective study of near-death experiences was published in the international medical journal *The Lancet*. The study was lead by cardiologist Pim van Lommel, MD, and set up in ten different hospitals in Holland over a period of 13 years. In this time period, 344 patients who had cardiac arrest were successfully resuscitated and they were then shortly after interviewed about their experience of being near to death. The study found that of the 344 patients, 62 patients or 18 percent reported having a near-death experience.[11]

This prospective study gives strong evidence that near-death experiences are not just stories that people make up, but that something does indeed happen to people who come close to death. Still, many experts remain skeptical. One attempt to explain the near-death phenomenon is that the experience is simply due to hallucinations brought on by the loss of oxygen to the brain, which in medical term is called "anoxia."

However, this explanation is a bit problematic because as we all know people who collapse or faint usually have total blackout or are at least very confused about what happened to them. But the near-death experiencer has a clear consciousness of the event, remembering the episode acutely for many years. So, the big question for the skeptics is; how can people have clear consciousness in a state of cardiac arrest with no brain activity (flat EEG)?

The best documented instance of this paradox is the case of Pam Reynolds. In 1991, Reynolds was diagnosed with a brain tumor and had to undergo very complex surgery called "hypothermic cardiac arrest." This is a procedure where the body temperature is lowered, the heartbeat and breathing stopped, the blood is drained from the body, and the brain waves are totally flat.

From 11:05 a.m. to 12:00 noon, Reynolds was clinically dead with flat EEG during the operation and in this timeframe she had a near-death experience. After coming back she was able to describe the instruments used during the operation and even conversations between the staff in the operating room. Both the instruments used and the conversations was later confirmed by the doctor and nurse.

Furthermore, her ears where plugged with a sound device that would make it impossible for her to hear anything. Dr. Spetzler, who carried out the operation, later said that, "At that stage in the operation, nobody can observe, hear, in that state...I don't have an explanation for it."[12]

The case of Pam Reynolds is not only a case of clinical death beyond reasonable doubt, but also provides a clear case of "veridical perception," where things seen or heard by the person during the NDE are later confirmed by others. In the study of veridical perception some studies have shown remarkable results. In one study of 16 cases, 88 percent of perceptions outside the body appeared to be accurate and 31 percent could be confirmed by objective means. In another study involving 93 cases, 92 percent appeared to be completely accurate with 35 percent being confirmed by objective means.[13]

Even with verifiable veridical perception as evidence there will be skeptics, and therefore, I have also examined my own experience from a skeptical point of view. I asked myself whether my episode could not simply be a recreation of input that I had collected subconsciously throughout my life, let us say from movies. But my experience was so real and so far beyond my own sensibilities that I do not see how I could have imagined it.

This is a common conclusion after the experience, and the International Association of Near-Death Studies (IANDS) tells us that people usually report that the experience is "hyper-real" and more real than the life we know in this dimension.[14]

Therefore, I have little doubt about the reality of my experience, and researcher Margot Grey confirms that this is typical: "To the near-death survivor there is seldom any uncertainty." One of her accounts describes this by saying that "there is no doubt in my mind that what I experienced was real."[15]

In his book *90 Minutes in Heaven*, Don Piper sums this up in a very good way:

> Before being killed in a car accident, I remained skeptical of near-death experiences. I simply didn't see how a person could die, go to heaven, and return to tell about it...These stories all seemed too rehearsed and sounded alike. Then I died, went to heaven, and returned...Not for an instant have I ever thought it was merely a vision, some case of mental wires crossing, or the result of stories I'd heard.[16]

In one study, *The Southern California Study*, "Ninety-six percent considered the experience real and not a dream, claiming that the contents of the experience were unlike anything they'd ever had in a dream."[17] One more thing to be said again in this relation is that the sense of realness stays with the experiencer. Usually people are able to recall the experience with perfect clarity many years afterward. In contrast, dreams and illusions are easier forgotten and disregarded as unreal.

This sense that the experience was real is also reflected by the aftereffects of the NDE, which are often deep and strong. P. M. H. Atwater, found that 79 percent were affected in a profound way, where 60 percent "reported significant life changes," while 19 percent "noted radical shifts—almost as if they had become another person."[18]

For me, this is certainly true about my experience also. The direction of my life totally changed after my experience to the extent that I would say I was reborn. Do dreams and hallucinations also have this strong life-changing effect? Having had both, and believing I know the difference, the answer is clearly, no.

Another researcher, Dr. Peter Fenwick tells us that, "[Near-death] experiences have a universal quality. If this were a purely psychological experience, one would expect it to be much more culturally influenced than it seems to be."[19] This is also the conclusion of Margot Grey, who puts the same point in the following way, "What has clearly emerged is that a common pattern of events, involving a sequence of occurrences that seem to be almost universal in their conformity of content."[20]

In *Lessons from the Light* by Kenneth Ring and Evelyn Elsaesser Valarino, Ring writes about his research into near-death experiences with blind people. Skeptics sometimes say that the NDE is created by conditioned images, or even that people must have seen the same movie about near-death experiences. It was this argument that Kenneth Ring wanted to investigate when he started to look for near-death experiences among blind people.

Interestingly, not only did he find that people who had poor eyesight could see clearly during the near-death experience, but he also found that some blind people were able to see for the very first time. In his study Ring found that 80 percent out of thirty-one blind people who had a near-death experience were able to see during their experience.[21]

Vicky, one person who had been completely blind from birth and survived two near-death experiences, explained, "Those two experiences were the only time I could ever relate to seeing, and to what light was, because I experienced it. I was able to see."[22] Another person, Brad, who had also been blind from birth said, "I know I could see and I was supposed to be blind...It was very clear when I was out. I could see details and everything."[23]

This gets even more interesting when Ring then wanted to compare their eyeless seeing with their dreams. When asked to compare their near-death experiences to their dreams, both Vicky and Brad answered that there were no similarity at all. The big difference is that blind people do not see things in their dreams like sighted people do.

Vicky tells us that, "I have dreams in which I touch things...I taste things, touch things, hear things and smell things — that's it." And when asked whether she was able to see anything at all during her dreams she answers, "Nothing. No color, no sight of any sort, no shadows, no light, no nothing."[24]

Brad explained the same, "I've had the very same consciousness level in my dreams as I've had in my waking hours. And that would be that all my senses function...except vision. In my dreams, I have no visual perceptions at all."[25]

Here are examples of two people who have never been able to see, but in their near-death experience are able to see for the first time. How is it possible for these blind people to transcend the sensory restrictions?

Kenneth Ring's explanation is what he calls *mindsight*—a transcendental awareness — that can be experienced as omni-directional perception through a 360-degree spherical vision that gives the near-death experiencers the ability to see with their consciousness.[26]

This description of seeing through consciousness is very much the same experience I had, and it is to be found in many other accounts. After leaving the body, one experiences another realm, and it is this realm that makes the experience more than real because this dimension is larger and more meaningful than this one.

Still, couldn't I just have imagined this other dimension? No, because in the same way that this dimension is indescribable, it is also unimaginable. I know that dreams are mostly extensions of reality and I also know what illusion or delusion is — they are distortions of reality. This experience of another realm, however, is neither. It is beyond our reality by being more real than anything in it.

The problem is that for someone who has not had the experience, to imagine something that is unimaginable is impossible. Therefore, disbelief seems to be a common response unless we already know or feel that there is something more to our universe.

Ring tells us that,

Something real, indisputably real, is happening to these experiencers...They are at once elsewhere but still here, in some sense with us...But, then, they are taken into an elsewhere to which we, the witness, can no longer have direct access...*another* reality.[27]

In trying to come up with a simple explanation confined within what we already know, I find that cardiologist, Pim van Lommel, agrees with my own conclusion from a medical viewpoint: "Our results show that medical factors cannot account for the occurrences of NDE...the near-death experience pushes the limits of medical ideas about the range of human consciousness and the mind-brain relation."[28]

I believe, as van Lommel is pointing towards, that the only scientific explanation for the near-death experience is to be found in the future study of consciousness. Based on my personal experience, I only see one way forward in explaining this anomaly, and it is by moving from the physical into the non-physical, and from the brain into consciousness. This is the only way we will ever discover the rest of the mystery 'out there,' and the true nature of the reality we live in.

Van Lommel also reminds us that there are cases of people who have awoken from a coma to tell that they were conscious during their coma. These cases are similar to the near-death experiences because the patients also left their bodies during their coma and were able to see their room and the people in it.

This introduces a similar phenomenon called death-bed visions or near-death awareness. These visions are experienced as dying patients get near to death and are very similar to near-death experiences. Many people report seeing the same kind of warm and welcoming light and also frequently attest to meetings with deceased loved ones.

Doctors, nurses, and palliative care workers all over the world have observed these experiences among their patients, and thereby, the evidence most certainly points towards some other kind of reality beyond the border of this life. It would seem that the near-death experience could be a very natural phenomenon that occurs quite naturally in a universe we know so little about.

Another question that I have asked myself is whether my experience truly is a proof that there is life after death. Does the possibility of consciousness *outside* the body mean that there can be consciousness *without* the body?

IANDS writes that, "There is no 'proof' in a statistical sense and no consensus of opinion. A more cautious explanation is that NDEs suggest that some aspect of the human consciousness may continue after physical death."[29]

However, IANDS also explains that scientifically, no means currently exist to demonstrate that this is true, and therefore, some people claim that near-death experiences are not scientifically 'real.' If what we call 'real' is only what we can measure, then this difference in opinion may come from the fact that the scientific method demands physical proof of reality.[30]

The main problem is, of course, that the near-death experience is subjective and therefore cannot be verified by others. This lack of 'real' evidence is mostly held by scientism, which has a strict material and almost fundamental view of reality. But if we ask the people who have had near-death experiences, we find very little doubt. IANDS tells us that, "Many near-death experiencers have said the term 'near-death' is not correct; they are sure that they were *in* death, not just *near*-death."[31]

Personally, I am convinced that I was *there*—in death, or as another person describes "there was nothing 'near' about it—it was there."[32] This distinction between *in* death or *near* death is an important distinction when we discuss whether or not there may be a continuation of consciousness after death. In her research, Margot Grey found that 76 percent of near-death experiencers had an increase in the belief in life after death.[33]

Kenneth Ring found that 91.2 percent of his accounts had a belief in life after death,[34] and he concludes that, "One of the strongest and most reliable findings from previous research in near-death studies is that NDEs tend to lead to an unassailable conviction that there is life after death."[35]

Thereby it is no wonder that the researchers of the near-death experience have the same belief. The father of the near-death experience, Dr. Raymond Moody, when asked if there is life after death, answered: "Yes, I concede that there is life after death."[36] Margot Grey holds the same opinion: "I am personally convinced we continue to have a conscious existence after physical death."[37]

Even though science is still skeptical of something that cannot be measured, this unassailable conviction of life after death is aligned with public opinion in America. A poll done by CBS News in 2005 found that 78 percent of Americans do believe in life after death.[38]

Leading researcher, Dr. Bruce Greyson, concludes from his 30-year long scientific research on the near-death phenomenon that, "We need to take the question of survival very seriously."[39]

Personally, I have no doubt that life continues after death and that consciousness can exist without the body. I think that the reason we cannot get any solid 'proof' is that we do not perceive all of reality. From my experience I am convinced that there is much, much more to reality than what meets the eye. Just as the universe continues beyond what we know, I am also convinced that life does.

William A. Tiller, physicist at Stanford University, has given what I believe to be the correct description of the scenario. "Humans see only a small fraction of the electromagnetic spectrum and hear only a small fraction of the sound spectrum. Perhaps we similarly perceive only a small fraction of a greater reality spectrum."[40]

Going Through the Experience

Let me begin by saying again that the near-death experience is truly beyond words. Therefore, each person who has this experience will give his or her own subjective interpretation of it. However, the experience, while being subjective, shares similar features that researchers call "core experiences." These basic features build a general understanding of the phenomenon.

In Raymond Moody's research, he found that the experience usually began with an extremely pleasant feeling at the very early stage of the experience. If a person had been in an accident, the pain would disappear and the person would be taken over by a peaceful sensation. Then some people experience what has been described as going through a tunnel till they find themselves out of their bodies.

The out-of-body experience takes people outside their physical bodies, allowing them to look down and see themselves. This is described as being "a spectator," or "a third person" in the room.[41] In most cases from hospitals, the view of the out-of-body state is placed near the ceiling, but in my case, as I was outdoors, I was looking down from a birds-eye view about ten to fifteen yards away. Another account explains leaving the body in a way that is similar to mine: "I was out of my body looking at it from about ten yards away, but I was still thinking, just like in physical life."[42]

In this state outside the body, some people describe having a transparent body and Moody calls this having a "spiritual body." At the same time other people describe this state of being as having no body at all, which is very similar to my own experience:

> They didn't feel that, after the release, they were in any kind of "body" at all. They felt as though they were "pure" consciousness.

One man relates that during his experience he felt as though he were "able to see everything around me—including my whole body as it lay on the bed—without occupying any space" that is, as if he were a point of consciousness.[43]

For me, it was like being space—as if I was pure consciousness—made of the structure of space. I left my body like a breath of air that went out of my body. One moment I was inside my body, the next moment I was outside this container that I was in just before. But there was no border crossing to leave my body, meaning that there was no tunnel I went through. It was more like a strong awakening: Now I am outside my body!

After having left the body, the most common core experience occurs, which is the encounter with the bright light. Seeing or entering this light is like entering another dimension or realm. In most cases there is a clear border between this world and this other dimension. One person describes: "It was beautiful and so bright, so radiant, but it didn't hurt my eyes. It's not any kind of light you can describe on earth. It is a light of perfect understanding and perfect love."[44]

Some people describe meeting deceased relatives, angels, or religious figures that act as guides for them in the light. Other people, like myself, experience being alone with or in the light. Meetings with religious figures seem to be conditioned by culture and are mostly considered highly subjective. Some researchers, therefore, find that the light itself is experienced as a form of being. Rather than God being personified, the light seems to be an expression of God in a broad sense—as the structure of existence and the whole universe.

However the light is expressed, the meeting with this unearthly dimension is an experience of love beyond human comprehension. Moody explains that the love and warmth that comes from the light is utterly beyond words.[45] Peter Fenwick, tells us the same thing, that, "This is nearly always an intensely emotional experience, so much so that often the experiencer cannot find the words to describe his feelings."[46]

In my experience it was like a sensation of an internal explosion, or expansion, of love that was more powerful than the sensation of free falling. With this extreme sensation came also the powerful revelation that the true nature of reality was infinite love, and in this state I had the experience of knowing the truth of the universe. I felt my consciousness expand to the size of the universe with all knowledge of all time.

Fenwick explains that the predominant quality of the light is that of bliss and universal love, but that it also "contains total knowledge."[47]

This is what before was described as "perfect understanding," and Moody says that many people describe the experience as "an entry into a higher state of consciousness or being."[48] With this experience of perfect love and understanding there is also a sensation of completeness or wholeness, as if one returns home to oneself. Many describe this as a "homecoming" or even "escape from jail."[49]

This makes the dimension of the light the best candidate for heaven that we have in human experience. Personally, I have no doubt that this experience is what we have been told about in the religions. However, rather than a physical place in the skies, it seems to me more likely that heaven is a state of being.

For me, this homecoming was the return to my true nature—not the self-centered person of my childhood and youth, conditioned by negative life experiences, but my nature the way I was meant to be: the ultimate state of my being. It was as if the light, the structure of reality, was the essence of my being, and this essence was the true nature of all existence. Another person testifies that, "This radiation of love entered me and instantly I was part of it and it was part of me."[50]

In this state there is no concept of time, and most people remark upon the *timelessness* of this out-of-body state.[51] It is as if the out-of-body experience takes you out the dimension of time and space that we know, and into another dimension—an infinite and boundless dimension—that is beyond our physical reality. All of these out-of-dimension elements make a good explanation why the near-death experience cannot be explained or proven in this world.

Then, at this point in the experience, some people experience what is called a "life-review." One account tells us that "The things flashed back came in the order of my life, and they were so vivid. The scenes were just like you walked outside and saw them, completely three-dimensional, and in color."[52]

This is a kind of flashback of one's life that is described as "a moment of startling intensity" being "incredibly vivid and real." The experience is so real that emotions and feelings associated to these images can be re-lived as one is seeing them.[53] For some people this is experienced as positive as they are reviewing positive episodes of their lives, while for others it is painful as their life-review display negative events in their lives.

In my experience, I had a negative life-review, which was very painful. Again, for me, if there is anything that I have experienced that could be a candidate for what we call "hell," then the negative life-review is it. However, in the near-death experience, the focus of the review does not seem to be to punish, but rather to focus on reflection so that the person can learn how to love.

Chapter Three

Religion

The belief that there is more to life than meets the eye is found among the vast majority of the population of the U.S.A. Polls show that 90 percent of Americans believe in God or some higher power.[1] This belief in a "higher power" illustrates what it means to be religious; Merriam-Webster's Dictionary defines the word *religious* as the "faithful devotion to an acknowledged ultimate reality."[2]

Personally, I strongly believe that the near-death experience is direct confirmation that such an ultimate reality does exist. Having had the experience confirms for me, beyond reasonable doubt, the existence of an ultimate reality. Therefore, I can understand why some researchers into the near-death phenomenon have suggested that most of the world's great religions were either started by or gained their inspiration from individuals who have had a near-death experience.[3]

Peter Fenwick tells us that, "Many people believe that in the NDE we are given glimpses of Heaven (or Hell). But it is just as reasonable to assume that it is the NDE itself which may have shaped our very ideas about Heaven and Hell."[4]

Many religions are built on the concepts of heaven and hell. Practitioners can gain a foretaste through the mystical experience, which in content shares some very similar features with the near-death experience. Fenwick, who sees the similarity to the mystical experience, explains that some of the common features are: intense realness, feelings of unity, feelings of joy and peace, and a transcendence of space and time.[5] Also Margot Grey tells us the same: "In my view, the perspective that offers the best possibility for attempting to understand the phenomenon (NDE) is that provided by the mystical teachings."[6]

So we find a great degree of resemblance between the near-death experience and the more mystical aspects of religion, in terms of both the belief in an ultimate reality and life after death. The skeptical argument towards religion is that religions are based on people's fear of dying, and that we therefore, create stories to make us feel safe.

To a scientific model solely based on the study of the physical world, this could certainly seem to be the case. But religion based on the mystical experience provides a source of inspiration rather than fear. In fact, the mystical experience is not only similar to the near-death experience; it is also very common.

One survey with a large sample of 45 million people in America found that 35 percent had had some form of mystical experience.[7] The fact that over a third of the population in the U.S. report having had a mystical experience argues for religion's basis in a positive belief in a higher power rather than just fear of the unknown. We also find that 46 percent, nearly half of the population in the U.S., say that they have "experienced God's presence or a spiritual force" many times in their lives.[8]

The Afterlife in Religion

The afterlife has always been the central topic of religion for many thousands of years, since the ancient times of the Shamanic cultures. In these very old cultures, probably dating back more than 80,000 years, the Shamans would send the spirits of the dead back to the stars. While modern man has cut himself off from nature, these ancient cultures were very deeply connected to both the natural and supernatural world, and this connection was used to guide their tribes.

The assumption that these cultures were childishly primitive is challenged today by new archaeological findings. Recently, shells from a pearl-like necklace were found in a cave in South Africa. Archaeologists believe that these remains date back 75,000 years, and they are thereby considered proof that our ancestors were thinking like us far earlier than what is widely accepted.[9]

Another good example of this is found in the interpretation of cave paintings. Until recently, it was believed that these "primitive" paintings were merely depictions of hunting animals, but new research show that the cave paintings are evidence of travels to the spirit world. These travels could be of a similar nature as the near-death experience, and therefore, it is possible that experiences of the ultimate reality are as old as humanity.

In Egyptian religion, we can find evidence of the ancient belief that when we die our spirit returns to our celestial home. Today we can still see the Great Pyramids the Egyptians built to help them ascend into the stars. In *The Egyptian Book of the Dead*, which is one of the oldest written sources we have today (about 1500 to 1400 B.C.), we find *The Doctrine of Eternal Life* and here we can get a sense of how the Egyptians saw their ascent into the heaven above:

> When Teta hath purified himself on the borders of this earth where Ra hath purified himself, he prayeth and setteth up the ladder, and those who dwell in the great places press Teta forward with their hands. In the pyramid of Pepi the king is identified with this ladder: Isis saith, Happy are they who see the father, and Nephthys saith, They who see the father have rest, the father of this Osiris Pepi when he cometh forth unto heaven among the stars and among the luminaries which never set.[10]

From this we only get a sense of where we go when we climb the ladder into the luminaries, but there is no direction of what happens there. This we find in another part of the text, which tell us that, "When the Osiris of a man has entered into heaven as a living soul...he walks among the living ones, he becomes God, the son of God."[11]

Here "the son of God," and before "the father" begins to sound like what we know from our Christian background. Even though there is talk about "a living soul," it seems that with embalmment and the need for "something" to climb a ladder, it would also hint that we could have grounds for the belief in resurrection of the physical body.

The Egyptians seem to have needed both a corporeal and incorporeal substance in order to reach the afterlife. In *The Egyptian Book of the Dead*, E. A. Wallis Budge points out that the Egyptian *ba,* translated "soul," is not only incorporeal because it dwells in *ka,* which is like the heart and possesses both substance and form.[12] With this Budge also tells us that, "it seems as if the Egyptians never succeeded in breaking away from their very ancient habit of confusing the things of the body with the things of the soul."[13]

In the East we find a much clearer distinction between the body and the soul. *The Bhagavadagita* in Indian religion tells us how to attain immortality in a way that fits with the near-death experience. *The Bhagavadagita* refers to "knowledge of the truth" as "knowledge of the relation of the individual self to the supreme."[14] It also tells us that it is with "the object of knowledge" that "one reaches immortality." [15]

This "object of knowledge" is referred to as the self, and the Bhagavadagita teaches that, "I am the self...seated in the hearts of all beings. I am the beginning and the middle and the end also of all beings...I am mind among the senses. I am consciousness in (living) beings."[16]

Now, the Bhagavadagita clearly makes the distinction between the body and the spirit, by explaining that the spirit is in the body: "The supreme spirit in this body is called supervisor...and the supreme self also. He who thus knows nature and spirit, together with the qualities, is not born again."[17]

The text then describes how we are to transcend above the elements (the qualities) that embody the self:

> When a right-seeing person sees none but the qualities to be the doer of all action, and knows what is above the qualities, he enters into my essence. The embodied self, who transcends these qualities, from which bodies are produced, attains immortality.[18]

Another text related to the Bhagavadagita, *The Anugita*, explains how the elements, or qualities, are the doer of all action: "From egoism, verily, were the five great elements born...In these five great elements, in the operation of perceiving sound, touch, color, taste, and smell, creatures are deluded."[19] The elements create a delusion through our senses, but when we die, "Every entity is dissolved into that from which it is produced."[20]

This transcendence of the elements is described in this way: "When, at the termination of the destruction of the great elements, the final dissolution [occurs]...the talented men who possess a good memory are not dissolved at all."[21] Here "good memory" is translated as knowledge of truth, and it connects us to the knowledge of self in the Bhagavadagita.

In the East, this intrinsic knowledge of self, or truth, is referred to as enlightenment. Relating this to my own personal experience, I have found that this Eastern interpretation of how to attain eternal life is, in fact, the most similar. The knowledge of self is what I experienced as my true nature, and the very idea that there is some kind of truth 'out there' seems to definitively be a very common feature of the near-death experience.

The similarity with the near-death experience is even more striking in Buddhism. Here we find *The Tibetan Book of the Dead*, or *The Great Book of Liberation (..)*, which is an in-depth instruction on how to attain eternal life through spiritual liberation. In *The Tibetan Book of the Dead*, liberation is attained by recognizing the "clear light" at the time of death: "Once they recognize the objective clear light, they will attain the birthless Body of Truth by the straight upward path without going through any between."[22]

The objective clear light is described as "an indescribable transparency, a light that is omni directionally illuminating yet beyond the brightness of sun or moon and also beyond dimness or darkness."[23] This is very close to the descriptions of the light in the near-death experience—clear, infinite, and stripped of all structure—and it empowers my conviction that the two are similar.

Enlightenment happens through one's identification with this clear light of infinite transparency, which recognizes the essential "selfless self."[24] The clear light and the selfless self constitute the true nature of reality, and Buddhism teaches that this absolute truth is the real essence of things. It is the ultimate nature and the main object of our realization.

The ultimate reality is characterized as being "indescribable, inconceivable, and unable to be signified by any word, gesture, or concept."[25] This is exactly the same characterization of the light that we find in the near-death experience, and the similarity between the two experiences is very striking.

The Resurrection

As I mentioned, it is clear that from my own experience, and those of many other near-death experiences, *leaving* the body does not mean taking the body with us. I am also confident that most people with a modern view on life after death do not literally believe in resurrection of the body, since the flesh actually rots and then there is nothing to return to. This materialistic understanding of resurrection is therefore in direct conflict with science and natural law.

Carl G. Jung once commented on this view by saying that, "To the primitive Christians as to all primitives, the Resurrection had to be a concrete, materialistic event to be seen by the eyes and touched by the hands, as if the spirit had no existence of its own."[26]

Instead of calling the early Christians primitive, I would say that it is probably more likely that the resurrection was inherited from Egyptian thinking, or some other source. In the New Testament, 1 Corinthians, Paul says: "If there is no resurrection of the dead, then not even Christ has been raised. And if Christ has not been raised, our preaching is useless and so is your faith."[27]

It is understandable how a literal interpretation of this line in the Bible can lead people to believe in bodily resurrection, since Christ being resurrected from the dead is central to Christian faith. However, right after this statement Paul says something that I believe to be even more important. Paul talks about being "false witnesses" and explains that those who have "fallen asleep in Christ are lost."[28]

On the topic of literal resurrection, I believe that in these times it is important to address the problem of fundamentalism. In my view, it seems that the Church has been holding on to its dogma for too long. A sign of this can be seen through scandals and rigid belief that has lead to the fall in church attendance over the last decades. Without disrespecting a strong tradition, as a philosopher I think that it is healthy to open one's mind to other possibilities, because holding on to dogma seems to be the wrong strategy in a world that is evolving.

One set of such other possibilities is contained in *The Gnostic Scriptures*, which was originally labeled as "heresy" by the church. This I find unfortunate since these texts give important second opinions that should be part of our reflection. It is even sadder to think of the long history where difference of opinion has lead to the killing of "the other" in the name of Christ.

In The Gnostic Scriptures we find *The Testimony of Truth*, which tells us that, "Do not expect, therefore, the carnal resurrection, which is destruction."[29] This view, dating back to about the second century, is very much aligned with modern science—the flesh dissolves.

The text is interesting, because it also has another view on why Adam and Eve where cast out of Paradise. It lets us know that, "The serpent was wiser than all the animals that were in Paradise, and he persuaded Eve, saying, 'On the day when you eat from the tree which is in the midst of Paradise, the eyes of your mind will be opened.'"[30]

The Testimony of Truth then boldly asks:

> Of what sort is the God? First he maliciously refused Adam from eating of the tree of knowledge. And secondly he said, "Adam, where are you?" God does not have foreknowledge; otherwise, would he not know from the beginning?[31]

Later the text answers the question of what sort of God this is by saying: "I am the jealous God; I will bring the sins of the fathers upon the children."[32]

In the East the serpent is not a symbol of evil, but the symbol of Kundalini energy. Kundalini is the *power of consciousness*, or supreme energy, also called mother of the universe. In Sanskrit the word means *"coiled up,"* and therefore, the symbol of a snake is the ancient symbolic representation, not of the devil, but of the supreme power of consciousness.

If we for example call the Kundalini energy for the Holy Spirit, then this could give us a different perspective on the words of John: "Just as Moses lifted up the snake in the desert, so the Son of Man must be lifted up, that everyone who believes in him may have eternal life."[33] In this interpretation it is the Holy Spirit as the power of consciousness that gives us eternal life.

In her book *The Gnostic Gospels*, Elaine Pagels, points towards the serpent as an *instructor* and she quotes from the text, *The Hypostasis of the Archons:*

> Then the Female Spiritual Principle came in the Snake, the Instructor, and it taught them, saying, "...you shall not die; for it was out of jealousy that he said to you. Rather, your eyes shall open, and you shall become like gods, recognizing evil and good."...And the arrogant Ruler cursed the Woman...and...the Snake.[34]

Here Eve, the "Mother of the Living," is a feminine spiritual principle that raises Adam from his material condition to bring him out of ignorance toward becoming like a God. It would seem natural to human nature (and historical correct) that arrogant male rulers would become jealous about this competition, whereby both the woman and the snake were cursed.

Through history, and even today, this curse has proven to be a powerful political tool of suppressing women with male aggression. And at the same time, the important question of personal identity has been left out. It seems logical to conclude that when these words were written around the second century, Gnostics saw the clear danger in the form that Christianity was taking as it became an organized religion.

In a modern day society, it certainly must seem good to most people that Adam ate from the Tree of Knowledge. I am sure that most of us are happy to be conscious and able to think for ourselves rather than being told what to think. In a democracy where everyone works together to solve the problems ahead, it is reasonable to give every individual the freedom to think.

However, the view of the Bible goes in the opposite direction, believing that "paradise was lost," which could be interpreted as ignorance is bliss, and I find it very interesting to note the negative direction. The Bible has a negative perspective from Adam and Eve being thrown out of paradise to the Book of Revelation—from paradise to the end of the world. This negative view on the world is also reflected through the views of "evil" and "sinners" that still today deserve punishment. The God of the Bible is an angry God that judges over irresponsible children living in an evil world.

The Gnostic perspective on the other hand is positive. It talks about ignorance instead evil, and sees a positive future through enlightenment and the gaining of knowledge. Surely such a view is far more optimistic than the pessimism of the Bible, and with a positive outlook on life it should be much more possible to create a positive future.

The Gnostics called the God of the Bible a "jealous God" because this God said: "I am God, and there is no other."[35] Looking at the history of the Church enforcing this one and only God, it is clear that this God has been much more angry than loving. We should not forget that the *Roman* Catholic Church was created on the foundation of the Roman Empire, after Emperor Constantine won the first battle in the name of the cross and Christianity later became the state religion of Rome. History also tells us that the doctrine of the Incarnation took root about the same time as Pope Urban II sent Christians of on the Fist Crusade with "God wills it!" After more than a thousand years of debate, in 1098 Saint Anselm published his *Cur Deus Homo*—Why God Became Man—and Jesus were since transformed from prophet into the one and only "son of God."[36]

Before we become upset at the past, it is worth taking into consideration that humanity has gone through a transformation as our thinking has evolved. Therefore, now that the children have become adults and outgrown their parents, I find it more important to ask where we should look for guidance. And as a philosopher, it is clear for me that we should look for truth by ourselves, and never accept someone else's truth. It was for this reason that Luther translated the Bible, so that we could all seek the truth by ourselves, instead of having it dictated to us.

It is not only possible but fairly easy to find other interpretations in the Bible that speak of an incorporeal resurrection. The Bible does in fact make a clear distinction between the body and the spirit. In 1 Corinthians we find: "I declare to you, brothers, that flesh and blood cannot inherit the Kingdom of God, nor does the perishable inherit the imperishable."[37] Also John gives the same interpretation of Jesus: "I tell you the truth, no one can enter the kingdom of God unless he is born of water and spirit. Flesh gives birth to flesh, but the Spirit gives birth to spirit."[38]

With this separation between the mortal and the immortal, Jesus uses the wind as a metaphor to describe the eternal spirit: "The wind blows wherever it pleases. You hear its sound, but you cannot tell where it comes from or where it is going. So it is with everyone born of the Spirit."[39]

In 1 Corinthians 15:40, we find that this distinction is made clear: "There are also heavenly bodies and there are earthly bodies; but the splendor of the heavenly bodies is one kind, and the splendor of the earthly bodies is another."[40] And this is made even clearer when the text continues: "So will it be with the resurrection of the dead. The body that is sown is perishable, it is raised imperishable; it is sown a natural body, it is raised a spiritual body."[41]

The Gnostic Scriptures offer an account that supplements this view of the Bible:

> If one does not understand how blowing wind came into existence, he will blow away with it. If one does not understand how body, which he bears, came into existence, he will perish with it...Whoever will not understand how he came will not understand how he will go.[42]

Gnosticism comes from *gnosis*, which means "knowledge" as opposed to *agnostic*, which means "not-knowing." Now, it can of course be argued that it is not humble to claim to know about the ultimate reality; an agnostic would say that we cannot know anything about this reality at all. Before my experience, as an atheist, I would probably have agreed with this view, but today after my experience, I believe like the Gnostics that we *can* know something about this ultimate reality. Just as my experience of this reality was the experience of my true self, so too does gnosis involve the process of knowing oneself—our true identity.

In a world where we are still in search of truth whether we believe it exists or not, I agree with the Gnostics that we should look for our own truth. For me, knowing our essence as our true nature is the ultimate reality and this is how we become resurrected in life and in death.

Pagels offer us this conclusion: "Only those who come to recognize that they have been living in ignorance, and learn to release themselves by discovering who they are, experience enlightenment as a new life, as 'the resurrection.'"[43]

She is thereby letting us know that,

> The "living Jesus" of these texts speaks of illusion and enlightenment, not of sin and repentance, like the Jesus of the New Testament.

Instead of coming to save us from sin, he comes as a guide who opens access to spiritual understanding.[44]

What is God?

Saint Anselm (1033-1109), bishop, philosopher and theologian, made an ontological assertion of God's existence: "God is that greater than which cannot be conceived."[45]

This description of God as something inconceivable is not far from the Buddhist indescribable and inconceivable ultimate nature.

The Bible begins with God's creation of heaven and earth in Genesis, telling us that, "God said: 'Be light made. And light was made. And God saw the light that is was good; and he divided the light from the darkness."[46]

Later in the Bible John reveals that, "In him (God) was life, and the life was the light of men."[47] Then we are told that there was a man, John, who came "to bear witness to the light," and this light "was the true light that enlightens every man."[48]

Through John we also learn that, "God is light,"[49] and that "God is love."[50] In this way, John gives testimony of God's nature by both explaining that the light is in God and that God is light 'himself.' This sounds a lot like the inconceivable light of love that is experienced in the near-death experience, and I believe that we are talking about the same thing here—that God is the source of the light. If God is not the nature of the light, then at least the light is part of God's nature.

The Gospel of Thomas has Jesus saying, "We came from the light, the place where the light came into being of its own accord and established itself...We are its children."[51] As children of divine light created in God's image, we also have the image of God within us: "He (Jesus) said to them...There is light within a man of light, and he lights up the whole world."[52]

In *Beyond Belief* Elaine Pagels explains that the big difference between The Gospel of John and The Gospel of Thomas is whether or not we have the image of God within us. John continuously reminds us that we (the people) cannot "recognize," or "receive" the true light, and this was why Jesus came to tell us about it.[53] Thereby, to those people "who believed in his name, he gave the right to become children of God."[54]

Pagels tells us that what John's gospel does, and has persuaded the majority of Christians to do, is that "only by believing in Jesus can we find divine truth."[55] She then says that Thomas' gospel on the other hand describes a Jesus that "directs each disciple to discover the light within."[56] Rather than John's "whoever does not come to me walks in darkness," Thomas lets Jesus reveal that, "The Kingdom is inside of you,"[57] and that, "You are from the kingdom, and to it you shall return."[58]

The conflict between John and Thomas is clearly whether or not we can realize God, or the light, by ourselves. With John it is only through Jesus that we can find God, whereas in Thomas' gospel we find the Kingdom of God within all of us. This is the difference between creating followers or independent individuals.

Thomas' Jesus also says that, "When you come to know yourselves, then you will become known, and you will realize that it is you who are the sons of the living father."[59] While John focuses on the need for the disciples to believe in the name of Jesus, Thomas' gospel clearly directs the disciples to find God for themselves, as they too, are sons of the father.

In the near-death experience we find evidence to support the view of Thomas' Jesus that the father lives within us all. Kenneth Ring calls this the experience of "being inwardly close to God," and he explains that near-death experiencers are more likely to shift in the direction of "God is within."[60] One account testifies that, "Everything that exists has the essence of God within it," and another tells us that, "I think that God is in every one of us; we are God."[61]

Finding the light within is what the East has been teaching long before the Bible was put together.

Before we looked at the descriptions of the Bhagavadagita, which said that, "I am the self...I am mind among the sense. I am consciousness in (living) beings."[62] This was the answer to the search for the source — the origin of the gods — which is the "creator of all things," and "lord of the universe."

The Anugita explains further that it is "by consciousness of self one enjoys the qualities; and thus [through] the source of all entities, the producer" that we come to know the creator of all things.[63]

The Bible does have descriptions that share similarity with this view: "One God and Father of all, who is over all and through all and in all."[64] And if we go back to the Old Testament, when God reveals himself to Moses on Mount Sinai we are told who God is: "I AM WHO AM...HE WHO IS."[65] In the footnote it is revealed that this I am who am means: "I am *being* itself."[66]

Still the Bible does not take us as far as I would like to go, which is why I find the Gnostic Scriptures so interesting. In *The Sophia [Wisdom] of Jesus Christ*, the text tells us that after Jesus rose from the dead, his twelve disciples *and* seven women were perplexed about "the underlying reality of the universe."[67]

In *The Sophia* Jesus tells his *19* disciples that,

> While they have inquired about God, who he is and what he is like, [they] have not found him...their speculation has not reached the truth...none is close to the truth, and they are from man. But I, who came from Infinite Light, I am here—for I know him [Light].[68]

The disciples ask for further clarification, and Jesus continues, "The Father is the beginning or principle of what is visible... the beginningless Forefather."[69] Phillip then asks how God appears to humans, and Jesus answers: "Before anything is visible, the majesty and the authority are in him, since he embraces the whole of the totalities, while nothing embraces him. For he is all mind."[70]

Then Jesus goes on to explain how creation appeared from mind:

> In the beginning, thought and thinkings appeared from mind...And from what was created, what was fashioned appeared. And what was formed appeared from what was fashioned...And after everything, all that was revealed appeared from this power.[71]

This interpretation of the nature of God is very modern and can be fit into our scientific understanding of the universe today. God as the principle of creation is very much like the search for what was before the big bang in science, and if we think of this principle being of mind as energy we can relate it to quantum physics and the study of consciousness.

Pagels lets us know that in Valentinian Gnosticism, God was "understood as the ultimate source of all being...an invisible incomprehensible primal principle."[72] Here she also refers to Protestant theologian Paul Tillich who talks about a "God beyond God." This *God beyond God* is the true nature of God as the "ground of being" that underlies all our concepts and images.[73]

Thereby, Pagels concludes that, "Achieving *gnosis* (knowledge) involves coming to recognize the true source of divine power—namely, 'the depth' of all being."[74] Here I see this "depth" and "ground of being" as fitting with the mind, consciousness, or the self. It is clear that if God is being itself—I am—then the true nature of God can only be found through realizing our true self, and not through others who tell us who or what God is.

To envision God beyond our literal interpretation is the way out of fundamentalism, and I believe that expanding our view of God as the ground of being can help us along in this direction. A modern understanding of God as consciousness, with the path to God seen as knowledge of the self, seems much more peaceful and aligned with the light on the other side than the fundamentalism many still practice today.

That God is fully knowable and that his words have been correctly interpreted in any book shows a lack of humility. The universe is beyond our understanding, and as Buddhism tells us, the ultimate reality is indescribable. We also find that the dimension of the near-death experience is beyond our comprehension.

The point in self-knowledge is that only we can realize our own true nature. No one can tell us our own truth; we have to find it by ourselves. The Bhagavadagita says of self-knowledge: "Neither the gods nor the demons understand your manifestation. You only know yourself by yourself."[75]

In her foreword to *The Gnostic Gospels*, Pagels quotes the Gnostic teacher Monoimus as saying the same thing.

Abandon the search for God and the creation and other matters of similar sort. Look for him by taking yourself as the starting point. Learn who it is within you who makes everything his own and says, "My God, my mind, my thought, my soul, my body."[76]

Chapter Four

Philosophy

During the time of the birth of western thought in ancient Greece, a split between two worlds happened. This split was symbolized by the disagreement between Plato and his student Aristotle. Plato had been the student of Socrates, who had been searching for the true nature of goodness. Carrying on this tradition from his teacher, Plato's thinking was founded on the ideal of the divine world. This transcendent immaterial world consisting of ideas, or forms, represented the true nature of goodness and indeed, the most real reality. In trying to reach this absolute reality, Plato's philosophy focused on the refinement of the soul.

Aristotle, however, did not agree with Plato that this ideal world was more real than the material world. Over time Aristotle is believed to have completely rejected the independent existence of Plato's objective reality.[1] Instead Aristotle focused his attention on the physical world through biology, and as a scientist, he brought philosophy down to earth. Some of us might know the famous fresco painting *The School in Athens* by Raphael, where Plato points up towards the heavens while Aristotle points down to the earth. This was not only the fundamental split between the immaterial and material world, but also the foundation of the split between religion and science that we see today.

As the Bible and classical texts were translated into Latin, so too was our thinking and the Church would later side with Aristotle, gradually rejecting the thinking of Plato. By the end of the 18th century, German philosopher Kant came with a sharp critique of Plato's pure reason and his world of ideas. Kant's philosophy caught on, and turned into what we today call critical rationalism. According to critical rationalism, life after death has been deemed "irrational," because it is outside our field of experience: "Death is the end of all experience."[2]

This belief is of course conditioned by the cessation of mental activity at the moment of death—something which the near-death experience suggests is not the case. But it shows us just how much the split has gone to the other extreme; to the scientist, the immaterial world is non-existent.

With critical rationalism and the advance of science, our western world turned materialistic. The Age of Enlightenment was supposed to make us enlightened, but it seems that this enlightenment only shines on the material world. Today we have to ask ourselves what caused our last century's record-breaking horrors? This problem in philosophy is called the path from the Enlightenment to the Holocaust—our material enlightenment led us to the systematic destruction of humanity.

It is very clear to me that this darkness comes from the lack of a moral foundation. Philosophy today has almost completely banished the notion of God, and the existence of a higher reality on which to focus the direction of our lives.

Sometimes it looks as if philosophy today is no more than a technique for debating, and from this point of view no topic is taboo. During my studies of philosophy at university, I remember a class where we calmly discussed the circumstances under which the torture of babies would be justifiable.

This question is deeply distasteful, but the fact that our class even discussed it supports my contention that the world seems to have become more relative. A recent national survey done by The Barna Group showed that Americans as a whole believe truth to be relative. Almost two out of three American adults, 64 percent, said that, "Truth is always relative to the person and their situation."[3] Only 22 percent said that truth is absolute. And the belief that truth is relative is even higher among teenagers. Here 83 percent said that, "Moral truth depends on the circumstances."[4]

The poll also found only a small gap in the belief in moral relativism between the generations. It showed that moral relativism was embraced by 75 percent of adults 18 to 35, and 60 percent of people 36 and older. Thereby the survey concluded that, "It appears that relativism is gaining ground, largely because relativism appears to have taken root with the generation that preceded today's teens."[5]

I understand the need to break free from the inflexible and dogmatic control of the Church, but I believe that freedom is not only unconditional. Because we are responsible for our actions, freedom is not free; it bears with it serious conditions and responsibilities. The argument for moral relativism is that if we cannot prove that moral values exist independent of human culture, then, moral values are relative. With this argument we can now justify any means by finding the right end. Today we call these means "the cost of war" when innocent children die for a "greater good." It justifies "the war on terror" to safeguard "freedom and democracy."

At the same time, it is almost too easy for us to disconnect from the impact of war when all we see are numbers. Human death and suffering are communicated to us through numbers, and depending on the race of humans, these numbers are relative. The currency of one American life is ten to one hundred times higher than the value of life in non-western countries. It almost seems like the mechanism that killed so many at Auschwitz is still alive and well.

Having experienced the indescribable nature of love in an immaterial world that lies at the essence of human nature, I am deeply horrified to see life placed at the mercy of a machine. If present day relativity reduces human nature to the inhumane, I feel that I must speak out about the deeper level of life that lies beyond our physical world. As the destructive teenager learns later as an adult that his or her actions do have consequences, so too, do the actions of humanity have consequences. And even though the teenager does not care about the consequences and believes that everything is relative, there is still truth beyond this way of thinking.

Roger Penrose, professor of mathematics at the University of Oxford, agrees with this point:

> People who take this relativist view think that, well, Einstein's relativity comes along and it completely overturns what we had before that we thought was true; it's all a matter of opinion and a social construct. I would say that, although there is an important influence from society, and although a lot of cutting-edge physical theories are tremendously fashion-driven, there is still a truth out there.[6]

If we say we believe all truth is relative, then we are affirming a truth which we do not believe to be relative, and we have contradicted ourselves. Philosopher William Desmond says that relativism has led to a sad conundrum: "The truth has been denied in favor of what is true *for us*." But ironically, he also tells us that, "The denial of truth cannot twist free of the embrace of truth. There is no escape from the true."[7]

We reject truth while at the same time we are looking for truth — whether we like it or not, truth is inescapable. While we cannot escape truth, the problem remains how to interpret truth, or as Desmond explains: "The difficult task is interpreting the metaphysical meaning of this necessity."[8]

The Platonic World

The truth 'out there' which Penrose talks about is the objective reality of the Platonic world. Plato's objective world consisted of divine values of both ethical and aesthetic truth. These are called *Platonic values,* and can be expressed by mathematical truth, goodness, justice, equality, harmony, beauty, etc.

Raymond Moody has suggested that the code of ethics and morals, including the higher knowledge from the Golden Age in ancient Greece, could have come from near-death experiences.[9] This suggestion, to me, is very likely. The Platonic values describe an absolute reality beyond our physical world, which Plato calls the *world of ideas.*

In *The Great Transformation*, Karen Armstrong points out that the Greek *idea* did not mean "idea" in English, but a "form, pattern, or essence."[10] That the Platonic values originates from a world of essence, or the essence of reality, does very much sound like the message from the near-death experience.

Plato himself explained that, "The good may be said to be not only the author of knowledge to all things known, but of their being and essence, and yet the good is not essence, but far exceeds essence in dignity and power."[11] That goodness in its essence far exceeds in dignity and power, the good we know in this dimension, fits very well with the "hyper-real" experience in the near-death experience. After the experience, people do not believe—they know.

This is also expressed by Carl Jung, who when asked if he believed in God, answered: "I do not need to believe. I know."[12] I should here mention that Jung himself had a near-death experience before this term was coined. I too, share this conviction—otherwise I would not be writing this—and my conviction is shared by many near-death experiencers.

The experience of "total knowledge" or "the answers to all the secrets of the universe," give testimony to this, and we also find accounts that testify to what Jung said: "If anyone asks if there is a God I shall say yes, I have seen him."[13] Another account tells us that, "Now I understood something more about God...that phenomenon experienced was God... that other afterworld is far more real than this one ever is."[14] Also Don Piper in *90 Minutes in Heaven* explains that, "*I know* I went to heaven...I *know* heaven is real. I have been there and come back."[15]

While it is not always possible for people to agree on exactly what God or heaven is, because our experience can only be explained through our subjective language, I am in no doubt that what our concepts point towards is very real.

But what is Truth? That is the big question that either troubles or haunts us all. According to Western logic, truth is that which is opposite to false, and with this world view we paint everything black or white. In stead of supporting this dichotomy, I will look towards the East again. Here the meaning of truth is ultimate reality of being—the fundamental reality underling everything that we see. In the same way that religion tells us that God is being itself, so we can here see Truth as the *truth of being*.

Going back to our Western roots, we find that the old Greek meaning of truth, "aletheia," concerns actuality as truth being opposite to mere appearance. Thereby, truth means "reality" as that which is true and real. Here the opposite of truth is unreal or as we just saw; mere appearance, and we do not find an aggressive rejection of its opposite in this Greek understanding of truth.

While being in itself is the absolute nature of being, our human interpretation of being is only the relative nature of being. Also the Eastern understanding does not reject the relative interpretation of truth as false, but rather searches for a deeper understanding of relative truth to reach the absolute truth. By not excluding its opposite, the Truth includes both its absolute and relative aspect.

In *The Fifth Element*, John Hick constructs a good definition:

> Truth is That which alone is, which constitutes the stuff of which all things are made, which subsists by virtue of its own power, which is not supported by anything else but supports everything that exists. Truth alone is eternal, everything else is momentary. It need not assume shape or form.[16]

In other words, truth is absolute, and what is experienced in the near-death experience points to the existence of such a truth. From these accounts it seems to be directly experienced that there exists an absolute reality beyond our physical world, which supports our relative reality. The world we see is only a part of a greater whole that has truth embedded in it.

As we are embedded in an unknown universe, we only see and understand part of the whole picture, but that does not mean that we can cut ourselves off from the full picture. In fact, the unknown out there pulls us towards it—or as William Desmond explains, the ultimate truth "opens up the promise of truth in the difference between itself and creation."[17] The difference between us and the unknown is what pulls us towards wanting to know about it, because we need to know in order to survive. Thereby, the ultimate truth is higher and more important than our relative physical truth because we are evolving beyond what we know into the unknown.

This is very much what Plato spoke about that the absolute reality was more important than our physical reality. Karen Armstrong lets us know that for Plato,

> The realm of the forms was thus primary, and our material world was secondary...The form (or essence) had an intensity of reality that transitory phenomena could not possess... its hidden essence...was more authentic than its earthly manifestation.[18]

The Truth outside the Cave

Coming back from meeting the light, I, like many near-death experiencers, found myself unable to precisely describe or put into words what I experienced. The light is experienced as truth, but after being experienced, this truth cannot be explained. The ultimate reality, being inconceivable, can only be experienced but not conceived.

Desmond explains that the *thatness* of the truth comes from a different kind of being, which has a determining source that itself cannot be determined.[19] This means that the truth is too big, and that we are too small to conceive or understand it. In other words, the created is too small to understand the creator.

The truth is so big, or bright, that Plato compares it to looking into the sun and being blinded by the power of its light. Instead we can glimpse the truth piece by piece, or little by little, as our eyes slowly get used to the light, and even so, we will never be able to make out the whole sun because it is too bright.

Penrose tells us that this is the same with mathematical truth:

> Once the idea has been grasped in essence, then the details may be examined afterwards. Imagine that whenever the mind perceives a mathematical idea, it makes contact with Plato's world of mathematical concepts. When one 'sees' a mathematical truth, one's consciousness breaks through into this world of ideas, and makes direct contact with it (accessible via the intellect).[20]

This is the same way that meditation works. When meditating, one's consciousness breaks through into the dimension of the light and an insight from the divine world is received. Then after the insight we need to contemplate and "examine the details." Plato told us that,

> The soul is like the eye: when resting upon that on which truth and being shine, the soul perceives and understands, and is radiant with intelligence; but when turned towards the twilight of becoming and perishing, then she has opinion only.[21]

When talking about fundamentalism, this point is very important. The light shines so bright that grasping the whole truth becomes impossible for the human eye. Still, what is important about this objective world is that it *communicates* truth. There *is* truth 'out there.' In the same way that a mathematician arrives at a mathematical truth, so too, does the Platonic world communicate or guide us towards an earthly truth. Just as there are physical laws, it is not difficult to see why there must also be laws of being—built-in laws of nature that guide life from its essence.

This connection between our physical world and the Platonic world is essential, because we are not disconnected from this truth. As we saw before, goodness is the essence and therefore the author of all things. This means that if we disconnect from our essence we also disconnect from the guiding author of our lives. It is this disconnection that makes it possible for man to commit such horrors against humanity—against his own true nature.

John Hick explains that, "When we speak of the ultimate goodness of the universe...we are talking about the total character of a reality which far exceeds what we can presently see and the physical sciences can ever discover."[22] This is how we, through ignorance, can destroy each other because we do not see the ultimate goodness that exists beyond our blind sight.

This total character of goodness is, from a material perspective, hidden to us because we do not perceive the immaterial world through our physical senses. Therefore, the whole truth or the full picture of reality cannot be experienced before the soul leaves the body. Plato told us that, much like in the near-death experience, when we leave the body at death we are able to see everything in its "true light."[23]

To see everything in its true light one must "become winged and fly up," to see what is there—"just as fish here leap up out of the sea and see what's here."[24] A fish is not able to understand the water in which it swims, and we are not able to fully understand the reality in which we 'swim,' either.

For me, being a fish that leaps out of sea to see what is there describes the out-of-body experience. Therefore, it sounds like Plato has actually been there, making Moody's suggestion very plausible. In fact, another story by Plato, about the soldier Er, is widely regarded as a story of a near-death experience. Plato lets Er explain that after his soul had left the body he came to a place where he could "see from above a line of light, straight as a column, extending right through the whole of heaven and through the earth, in color resembling the rainbow, only brighter and purer."[25]

Plato's Cave allegory also reminds me of the near-death experience. In this story he describes how some prisoners are chained up inside a dark cave. Their reality consists of shadow images from a fire within the cave, and they have no knowledge what so ever about what is outside the cave. Plato explains that "the truth would be literally nothing but the shadows of the images," and that in this shadow world of illusions the prisoners inside the cave would be engaged in the ridiculous competition of measuring the shadows.[26]

Then one day, one of the prisoners escapes his chains and goes towards the exit of the cave. And there, Plato asks,

> If he is compelled to look straight at the light, will he not have a pain in his eyes which will make him turn away to take refuge in the objects of vision which he can see, and which he will conceive to be in reality clearer than the things which are now being shown to him?[27]

Plato here points to the paradox of the prisoner's inability to perceive, and worse, to explain, what he has just seen outside the cave. He has only the conception and language of the shadow-world to achieve this, and they are painfully inadequate. This is the same paradox the near-death experiencer faces—how to express the indescribable nature of the experience.

Plato tells us that the prisoner will have to grow accustomed to the sight of the upper world, and after some observation and reflection he will be able to comprehend. For me, the light of the world outside my body was exactly like this—too bright. Therefore, it took me long time adjusting to the light, and learning what the reflections of the light look like in this world.

Having been outside the cave, it is only natural to want to tell others about what is there, and this is also what the freed prisoner is motivated to do. After having comprehended the truth outside the cave, the freed prisoner, out of compassion, feels the need to free the other prisoners. However, this will prove even more difficult, since they are too conditioned by their shadow world, and the story ends with the other prisoners killing their liberator.

This is with little doubt the same human mechanism that got Jesus killed, as he was also trying to liberate humanity. Plato makes this clear by saying that "you will not misapprehend me if you interpret the journey upwards to be the ascent of the soul into the intellectual world."[28]

Plato also reveals that our prison, our cave, is "the world of sight," or what can call sense data. The material world that we experience through our senses is our dark cave, and this is why we deny the existence of the immaterial world, because we do not receive any data of its existence through our senses. Aristotle and the scientism of today do not want to know what is outside the cave, and therefore they cling to the shadows. But we all have to die one day, and when we do, we will see what is outside the cave.

To think that there is nothing outside is ignorance, and a fundamental mistake because the outside is connected to the inside. The outside is the inside of the cave in its true nature. The outside, our immaterial essence or soul, is the way out of the darkness of the cave. But to leave the cave we must first have faith that there is an outside of the cave in order to look for the exit.

So, to escape the cave we need to understand that there are two substances: The material and immaterial. In philosophy we call this the soul-body duality, or mind-body problem. This problem is still unresolved, or disagreed upon, and has become ever more pressing recently in light of modern science's search for the answer to the creation of Artificial Intelligence.

For Plato, this problem was solved by explaining that death and life are two different substances: "When death comes at a human being, his deathbound part, as is likely, dies, but his un-dying part takes off and goes away safe and undestroyed."[29] This is possible because the "soul doesn't admit death," and what does not admit death is immortal.[30]

However, this duality of life and death is more complex. Plato told us that "there's the thing itself that brings some contrary to bear,"[31] meaning that the word "death" brings a contradiction in itself. There are "simple fractions" that cannot "admit the idea of the Whole,"[32] and this leads to the ultimate point that there is no duality at all. Life and death are not separate because there is no death. Life does not come from death—life comes from life—it is already there and it does not go anywhere.

From this perspective, the word and the conceptual understanding of "death," is the thing that brings a contrary to life. The concept itself is a separation from life, and so, there is no death, only the misconception of the separation from life. Therefore, life as the idea of the whole cannot admit death, because death is the illusion that creates the separation from the whole.

This is expressed in modern words by Eckhart Tolle in *A New World*. Here Tolle explains that the separation between "life" and "my life," is an illusion created by the ego. He then unties the separation in a plain and simple way: "There is no such thing as 'my life,' and I don't *have* a life. I *am* life. I and life are one."[33]

Finally, with life being eternal, Plato let us know the consequence of the illusion of death:

> If the soul is indeed deathless, she's in need of care, not only for this time in which we call 'being alive' goes on, but for time as a whole; and the risk now would seem to be dreadful, if somebody is careless of his soul. For if death were freedom from time as a whole, it would be a godsend for bad men, who in death would be at once set free.[34]

Descartes' Path to the Soul

In the 17th century, French philosopher René Descartes showed the way to the Platonic world within—our eternal undying part of the soul or mind. This is a key part in trying to understand how life can continue, because it is important to know exactly what it is that continues. For me, having left my body to become pure consciousness has given me the conviction that this is how life continues—through disembodied consciousness.

In separating the body and the mind, René Descartes delivered his big contribution to the Age of Enlightenment. He explained that enlightenment happens within God, not outside or out from God. Basically, this meant that people had to think for themselves in order to find the truth.

In *Meditations on First Philosophy*, Descartes shows the path to our true identity, and to lead us to our true identity he demonstrates "the distinction between the body and the soul." In making this distinction the body-soul duality took root in Western philosophy.

It is popularly believed that Descartes was only seeking to rebel against the control of the Church by leading us to our true identity. But separating the body from the mind not only shows us who we are; it also leads to an understanding of how we enter the afterlife. For me, it is very clear that true identity and eternal life are two sides of the same coin because our true nature is eternal.

In the *Meditations* Descartes tells us that the foremost important "prerequisite for knowing that the soul is immortal is that we form a concept of the soul that is as lucid as possible and utterly distinct from every concept of a body."[35] Separating the soul from the body becomes central to immortality, because "the annihilation of the mind does not follow from the decaying of the body (and thus these considerations suffice for giving mortals hope in an afterlife)."[36]

In order to direct the mind towards itself, Descartes leads us away from the senses. He does this by bringing sense perception into doubt:

> Whatever I had admitted until now as most true I received either from the senses or through the senses. However, I have noticed that the senses are sometimes deceptive; and it is a mark of prudence never to place our complete trust in those who have deceived us even once.[37]

The doubt of sense data leads him to the one thing that is doubtless: "I am; I exist—this is certain."[38] There is truth within existence, and therefore, Descartes pointed towards our truth within, which is our true identity. This method of Descartes leads the mind to its own nature through the question: Who am I?

The question of who we are is the key to understanding the difference between the body and the soul. Believing that the part of ourselves which we identify as "I" is equivalent to the body is too simple, because where exactly do we find this "I"? The "I" is that which thinks and Descartes concludes that I am "a thinking thing."[39] Thereby, to think is the essence of our nature—thinking is at the center of our being—and it is this thinking function that characterizes the concept of "I."

The "I" as a thinking thing is the clear distinction between the body and the soul. Descartes defines "I" as mind, intellect, understanding or reason. The essence of the "I" is to be aware; modern terminology would call it conscious. Consciousness—being conscious—is our true identity. Knowing our true identity is not only important in finding our own truth, but our true identity also carries us safely into the afterlife. Without the knowledge of who we are, there is no stable foundation on which to stand when we enter what comes after life.

Consciousness is now the center of our being, or the first cause of being, as we *are conscious* before we are conscious *about* something. There is nothing before and there is nothing after, since this state is eternal: "I suppose that perhaps I have always existed as I do now, as if it then followed that no author of my existence need be sought."[40]

Descartes explains why the soul or consciousness is eternal. By making the distinction between the body and the soul, he also makes the distinction between the material and the immaterial. The body and all physical objects are material and extended in space, while the "I," consciousness, is not extended in space. Here, Descartes shows why science cannot find the source of consciousness—the "I" is not extended in space.

Not being extended in space leads to the conclusion that being outside space consciousness is also outside time. Time and space define the physical dimension in which consciousness is nowhere to be found, and therefore, consciousness is beyond both time and space. This is Descartes' argument for eternal life, and comparing this to my own experience, and the evidence left to us by the near-death research, it does seem to be very correct.

In the separation of material and immaterial there is a fine line. Descartes also tells us how we create "material falsity," when we let our ideas represent "a non-thing as if it were a thing."[41] This can be seen in the case of fundamentalism, which makes our ideas solid and hard as material things. When we say: "I *am* my body," or "I *have* a life," it is the same material falsity that Tolle speaks about when we say *"my* life" instead of *"life."* These ideas are material falsities because we judge an immaterial thing to be a material thing. Here Descartes would say, "I exist—I am mind," and this is the same statement as *I am life*.

In pointing out our true identity through separating our body and mind, Descartes is blamed for creating duality in our Western world. Of course duality directly conflicts with Western logic, which says: either/or. This creates great problems for the Western mind, because it is forced to choose one of the two. Today the choice has fallen on the material world as we have rejected the immaterial world.

But duality does not have to be so black and white that some of us make it out to be. On the body-mind issue Descartes himself actually unites the two parts. In the last meditation, after having separated the mind from the body, he puts them back together:

Nature also teaches not merely that I am present to my body in the way a sailor is present in a ship, but that I am most tightly joined and, so to speak, commingled with it, so much so that I and the body constitute one single thing.[42]

The mind and body are expressed by "the union" that is the "commingling of the mind with the body."[43] So really, the outside and the inside are not separate, but united as one single thing. Having established each part's existence, they have to be united again in the right balance.

It seems that Descartes' intention behind his separation of the body and the mind was to point out the distinction between the dying and un-dying parts of our existence. Knowing our true identity gives us the keys to the afterlife and opens the door to eternal life. In chapter six, I will look deeper into this issue in order to open the door for those who are not yet sure where to step on the other side.

Descartes also told us that eternal life is supported by physics. He says that,

The premises from which the immortality of the mind can be inferred depend upon an account of the whole of physics...absolutely all substances, that is, things that must be created by God in order to exist, are by their very nature incorruptible, and can ever cease to exist.[44]

How eternal life can be explained through science is what we will look at in the next chapter. From the perspective of the near-death experience, I will look into the scientific understanding of our universe to find where it matches my own personal experience.

Chapter Five

Science

In the previous chapter, we learned from philosophy that what we perceive through sense data it not all there is to reality. As in Plato's allegory of the cave, our senses only reveal a shadow-reality to us, while the full picture and the whole truth await us outside the cave. This was also the view of Carl Jung, who said that, "Reason sets the boundaries far too narrowly for us, and would have us accept only the known—and that too with limitations—and live in a known framework."[1]

Reason is governed by logic and therefore, we can say that the limit of our logic is the border of our world. But as we have seen before, when the earth was believed to be flat, new understandings were required to expand our borders beyond the logic of the past. This brings us back to William A. Tiller again, who said that perhaps we only perceive a small fraction of a greater reality spectrum.

My mystical experience left me totally blown away in awe over what lies beyond logic. Basically, the logic of science sets up very simplistic material models into which we expect all of reality to fit. This is not possible because the universe is too big, and again and again, science must expand its views and models to keep up with the changing paradigms.

For example, it was once believed that everything 'real' was made up of matter. Science now estimates that what we know as matter only makes up about four percent of our universe. The rest of the universe scientists call dark-matter and dark-energy, but the truth of the matter is that they do not know what this other dark stuff in our universe is. Tiller was right—about 96 percent of our universe is unknown.

It also means that we do in fact live in a dark cave, ignorant about what is outside. The limits of our world—what we through our senses see and define as our physical world—is only a small fraction of a greater reality. The perceivable limits of our world are still what we see and what we can understand through logic, but there is more—much more...

The Birth of a New Dimension

In the 1920's, science saw the birth of quantum physics, which lay the framework for a whole new way of understanding our physical universe. Through scientific experiments with light particles, something big happened; through the so-called *double-slit experiment* it was shown that the particle of light, the *photon*, both had particle and wave features. This lead to the conclusion that, "*all* matter has a wave-like character,"[2] which means that all matter is essentially energy.

Thereby quantum mechanics gave birth to the *wave-particle duality*, a radical and new understanding of our universe, in which our material reality was joined by an immaterial reality. Now science had discovered and *proven* the existence of a non-material dimension of reality that co-exists with our material dimension of reality.

The discovery of this non-material universe does have serious consequences for the way we view the world and especially for our either/or logic. According to conventional logic, one thing cannot be more than one thing at a time, and so, matter has to be either matter or energy—it cannot be both. But in fact it is, which illustrates the duality of both/and because our physical world is both particle and wave—both matter and energy at the same time.

In essence our universe is a hidden world of energy fields in vibration, and these energy fields are in constant change through interaction by the exchange of energy. It is because this interaction is in constant movement that there is no stabile matter. So, when we say that the physical reality is true, we have to be careful because in essence— absolute truth—there is no matter.

Quantum mechanics reveals that it is the intensity of the energy that attracts and makes the particles of the body come together. When the attraction is so great that the particles interact and 'touch,' they become matter, and it is in this way that the density of the energy make up the physical body. Then through the interaction of energy the senses come alive and we start to feel, hear, see, and touch.[3]

The reason that the body seems solid and physical to us is explained in almost the same way that the projection of film works. In a movie the rapid succession of 24 still pictures per second produce the illusion of movement. In the same way, the energy in vibration collapses about 40 times per second to form our illusion of solid matter. The way to understand this is that the vibration is so fast that the energy seems solid to us, while it is actually not.

The energy can neither arise nor fade away, which means that it can neither be born or die. The energy is constant in eternal existence, and can never come out of existence. As Descartes told us before, all things created by God are incorruptible, and so, the energy can never die. It only changes through interaction and exchange, and in this way there is no death of this energy. The energy only changes form by transforming into new particles.[4]

From this point of view, our fundamental nature is pure energy, and when we die we return to our true nature—pure energy. This scientific explanation fits very well with *The Anugita*, which before told us that, "When, at the termination of the destruction of the great elements, the final dissolution approaches and every entity is dissolved into that from which it is produced."[5]

More Dimensions of Reality

Quantum physics later evolved into what we today call String Theory, which emerged in the 1980's. Since then this theory has been the most successful theory in predicting the outcome of scientific experiments. It is regarded as the most successful theory in the history of science, and its conclusions are radically changing the way scientists view our universe.

One of these predictions is that our universe has seven extra dimensions of space than the three we know of already. These extra dimensions support Tiller's claim that our three dimensions of space are only a fraction of a greater reality, and it is within these extra seven dimensions that we find the 96 percent of unknown material in our universe. As dark matter and dark energy are invisible to us, so this immaterial universe of extra dimensions is also hidden to us.

The theory explains that the original state of a ten dimensional universe was unstable, and for this reason the universe broke into two pieces; our three dimensional universe (plus the dimension of time), and a seven dimensional sister universe.[6] This means that our four dimensional reality is only a fraction of the larger eleven dimensional universe, and therefore, we do in fact only perceive a fraction of reality.

So, why do we not see these extra dimensions? They are made of tiny strands of energy that are so small, they are hidden to our sight. In *The Elegant Universe*, physics professor Brian Greene tells us that, "Since strings are so small, not only can they vibrate in large, extended dimensions, they can also vibrate in ones that are tiny and curled up."[7]

Fundamentally, we cannot see strings because we cannot see energy. We all talk about energy and we can feel the energy of other people even though we cannot see it. One example of this invisible universe is the world of mobile telecommunication. Imagine all the telephone conversations going through the air in New York City over the course of one second. In the same way that conversations occupy our space invisibly, so too does energy. When we move our hand through the air, we not only move it through the three space dimensions that we can see, but also through the tiny extra dimensions (and all the telephone calls).

Trying to imagine more dimensions is almost impossible. Our mind is set on a three dimensional space through our senses, and so, to imagine a universe of four space dimensions is very difficult. I believe that this is the same reason that the near-death dimension is so difficult to explain after returning from it.

It is easier for us to imagine fewer dimensions, for example, a universe made up of only two space dimensions. A two dimensional space would not have front and back, only left and right, up and down, and thereby it would be a completely flat dimension like a piece of paper. Imagine what it would be like to live in a two dimensional universe and then be suddenly projected into a three dimensional universe for the first time. Now, try explaining this to your two dimensional friends! You would have the same problem as someone who has had a near-death experience.

The Out-of-Dimension Experience

With all of these discoveries in new science, it means that we can now begin to understand the near-death experience from a scientific viewpoint. Brian Greene asks us to imagine a raw state of existence beyond which energy has not been organized into the form that we see as space-time:

Imagining such a structureless, primal state of existence, one in which there is no notion of space or time as we know it, pushes most people's powers of comprehension to their limit...Nevertheless, it is likely that we will need to come to terms with such ideas and understand their implementations before we can fully assess string theory.[8]

To me, it seems very likely that what science is here trying to reach is the dimension of the near-death experience. Because it is the experience of a different dimension than our four dimensional space-time universe, I choose to call it the *Out-of-Dimension Experience*. This is to make clear that instead of hallucinations of the mind, the out-of-dimension experience does in fact describe a different dimension as quantum physics predicts.

In another book, *The Vibrating Universe*, N. C. Panda asks the question:

Can we directly have an experience of the hidden constant? If and when we do that, we indeed become that hidden constant. It no longer becomes hidden to us. There are no 'It' and 'we', no 'that' and 'I', no 'you' and 'I', no subject and object.[9]

The answer for me is: Yes—the out-of-dimension experience is the experience of this hidden constant as a structureless and primal state of existence. But just as science has difficulty locating this ultimate state of existence, so too has the out-of-dimension experiencer difficulty with both proving and explaining it. Panda says that this ultimate reality "can be directly or immediately experienced. But, even after it is realized or experienced, it cannot be expressed in language."[10]

People who have out-of-dimension experiences would agree. "There was no separateness at all. I can only say that I believe that I was in a state of total cosmic consciousness. I felt tremendous peace and oneness; the unity was indescribable."[11] Another person reveals that the light "totally absorbed my consciousness. It seemed to radiate from the very center of the consciousness I was in and shine out in every direction through the infinite expanses of the universe."[12]

Raymond Moody also found evidence of this. He tells us: "They [experiencers] got brief glimpses of an entire separate realm of existence in which all knowledge—whether of past, present, or future—seemed to co-exist in a sort of timeless state."[15]

To explain how the out-of-dimension experience is possible from a scientific viewpoint, we have to look towards what quantum physics call *phase transition*. Phase transition explains how a substance can change form from one state to another through the transition. One example is the transition of ice into water, and water into steam.

Physicist Brian Greene notes,

> The kinds of black holes we were studying and elementary particles are actually two phases of the same underlying string material...we see that black holes and elementary particles, like water and ice, are two sides of the same coin.[16]

We all know that solid ice, when it melts, goes through a phase transition and changes into water. In the same way, we can explain that our being—our essence—goes through a black hole (phase transition) as it leaves our body and is released as pure energy. Our physical experience of this dimension and the energy are not separate any more than ice and the water are; they are two sides of the same coin.

If we now imagine the universe as an ocean of energy, then this is where we return to as "water" after going through the transition of the black hole. Gravity is bound up with space and time, or we could say that gravity holds our dimension together. Quantum physics reveals that gravity is made up of particles called "gravitons," and these can be either tied down with matter or they can also be in a free state as "free gravitons."

These free gravitons are able to "escape" our dimension and enter into other dimensions. We could say that as the gravitons are released from the body, both time and space dissolve, which would explain why the out-of-dimension experiencer does not experience time. And to take another guess in the interest of investigation, it could even be that the graviton release causes a sensation of gravity, as some people in out-of-dimension experience describe a sensation of "free falling,"[17] or "rushing through space at a great speed."[18]

For me, it was a very powerful sensation as; maybe my gravitons were being released!

Interconnected Universe

In 1964, the Irish physicist John Bell made what has been called "the most profound discovery of science." Certainly in my view, this scientific discovery will have deep future implications on the way we view our world. Bell's discovery and prediction lead to the Aspect experiment two decades later, which confirmed the existence of quantum entanglement—the proof that "an object over there does care about what you do to another object over here."[19]

In 1997, a replication of the Aspect experiment was carried out by Nicolas Gisin and his team at the University of Geneva. The original Aspect experiment had been performed at a distance of 13 meters, but now the two detectors were placed 11 kilometers apart. Due to the small size of the photon, this might as well be at a distance of 11 million kilometers—or even 11 billion light-years.[20]

These experiments proved that "the two photons are so intimately bound up that it is justified to consider them—even though they are spatially separate—as parts of one physical entity."[21] Photons, it turns out, are able to communicate instantaneously over vast distances, and this means that the particles are connected outside of space and time. This leads us to the astonishing conclusion that the particles are connected beyond the world as we know it—a concept that is difficult for science to conceive. As Brian Greene inquires, "What does it really mean to say two spatially separate things are one?"[22]

Most conservative scientists are reluctant to conclude that this means that everything is connected and that quantum entanglement makes everything in the universe one. But for now, it is enough for me to have physicists claim that particles may be "so intimately bound up that it is justified to consider them as part of one physical entity." Whether or not this proves that all things are one, this scientific conclusion fits perfectly with the experience of oneness and completeness in the out-of-dimension experience.

Here the feeling of interconnectedness is expressed as: "I had no sense of separate identity. I was in the light and one with it."[23] Another experiencer reveals that, "There was no separateness at all...I felt tremendous peace and oneness, the unity was indescribable."[24] A third person tells us that, "This radiation of love entered me and instantly I was part of it and it was part of me."[25]

In the out-of-dimension experience we can also say that a teleportation of thoughts takes place. People are able to "pick up the thoughts" of others—not from any voice or sound, but "rather, it is reported that direct, unimpeded transfer of thoughts takes place."[26] This transfer of thoughts is a form of communication with "perfect understanding" where one becomes "instantaneously aware."[27]

To some people teleportation of thoughts might sounds very mystical, but also in 1997 two groups of physicists carried out the first teleportation experiments. The experiments successfully carried out the *teleportation* of a single photon, and it was shown that quantum entanglement can be used for quantum teleportation.[28]

The teleportation of particles through quantum entanglement lead to the beginning of the development of quantum computers, which will be able to teleport information from one computer to another, instantly, beyond time and space. These computers are in the making as I am writing this, and recently, *New Scientist* magazine announced that, "Now is the realistic possibility truly emerging."[29]

The development of quantum computers has been funded in order to create greater security in the use of computers through *quantum cryptography*. Designed to encode and decode messages, this secret quantum key works on quantum entanglement, where the particles are linked even when they are far apart.

Can it be that we are now able to develop computers, which prove through the way they operate that things are not separate? Particles are connected through entanglement and this interconnectedness in now being used in science. If interconnectedness is a law of nature, proven by science, then we have to begin asking ourselves about the consequences of our actions.

The out-of-dimension experience clearly suggests that our actions impact others and that we will experience the consequences of this. Near-death researcher Pim van Lommel calls the recollection of one's past in the out-of-dimension experience the Holographic Life-Review, because all our actions and thoughts are stored in a holographic field of consciousness. Through quantum entanglement, or non-locality, everything is interconnected, and in the out-of-dimension experience, we thereby connect to our own field of consciousness as well as those fields of other people—all the fields are interconnected and everything is stored.[30]

Absolute Reality

Now, the question arises whether reality 'out there' is absolute or relative? To answer this I believe it is relevant to go back and see what Einstein actually meant by relativity. Brian Greene reveals that,

> Einstein's theory does not proclaim that everything is relative...for this reason Einstein did not suggest or particularly like the name "relativity theory." Instead, he and other physicists suggested

invariance theory, stressing that the theory, at its core, involves something that everyone agrees on, something that is *not* relative.[31]

In the out-of-dimension experience there is an experience of an absolute or ultimate reality, which is experienced as the true nature or structure of the universe. Peter Fenwick says that "with the peace often comes a feeling of profound knowledge, a realization that you have been given the answer to all the secrets of the universe."[32]

One near-death experiencer tells us that: "I was peaceful, totally content, and I understood I was born on earth and knew the answer to every mystery—I was not told, I just knew, the light held all the answers." Another account lets us know that,

> All around me were the answers to everything, no puzzles because I had been given the key to understand everything. What was so thrilling was that the perfect, logical simplicity convinced me that only the Creator could have made it so...Enlightenment is the wonder, and here I understood the universe.[33]

The evidence of an absolute reality is what we already find in mathematics. Numbers seem to be absolute and independent of subjectivity because numbers are objective, which makes them true and absolute. What makes numbers real and true is that they seem to have a life of their own, and this life of their own, as we saw before, is an existence that takes place in the Platonic world.

Roger Penrose explains that,

> When mathematicians communicate, this is made possible by each one having a *direct route to truth*, the consciousness of each being in a position to perceive mathematical truths directly, through this process of 'seeing'...The mental images that each one has, when making this Platonic contact, might be rather different in each case, but communication is possible because each is directly in contact with the same externally existing Platonic world![34]

One of the most magnificent things in mathematics is the Mandelbrot Set. This set of numbers (an equation), which creates an unending geometrical shape, has been called "The Thumbprint of God."[35] This new field in mathematics is called fractal geometry, and what is interesting about it is that it seems that there is a connection between the Mandelbrot set and the way nature operates.[36]

About the set, Penrose lets us know that,

It would seem that this structure is not just part of our minds, but it has a reality of its own...The Mandelbrot set is not an invention of the human mind: it was a discovery. Like Mount Everest, the Mandelbrot set is just *there*![37]

Another scientist, Dr. Michael Barnsley, tells us that, "The Mandelbrot Set is real. An absolute thing—no question whatsoever!"[38] He then says that the Set is a hidden seed exactly like DNA, "a little formula that is unraveled by the process of growth and deterministic following of rules to form this natural and beautiful thing."[39]

That the universe seems to operate on given laws is what science proves to us. By understanding the laws of our universe we discover the inner workings of nature, and since the dawn of science it has been believed that the universe had an ultimate structure. From the time of Aristotle there has been a term in science named "luminiferous aether," or just *aether*, which was used to describe the ultimate nature of the universe as *unseen light-carrying stuff*.

About this light-carrying aether, Greene lets us know that, "Many physicists viewed the aether as a down-to-earth stand-in for the divine spirit that Henry More, Newton, and others had envisioned permeating absolute space."[40] And today in modern science, "key developments in modern physics have reinstituted various forms of an aetherlike entity."[41] This means that the concept of "divine spirit" as the ultimate structure of the universe, which one would normally associate with religion, is not that alien to science.

Greene tells us further, as a scientist, that,

Without invoking the spiritual, therefore, we may well closely brush up against the thinking of Henry More in our scientific quest to understand space and time. To More, the usual concept of empty space was meaningless because space was always filled with divine spirit. To us, the usual concept of empty space may be similarly elusive, since the empty space we're privy to may always be filled with an ocean of Higgs field.[42]

The Higgs Field in science shares similarities with the concept of divine spirit, and in the same way that the spiritual world is hidden to us, so is the world of the Higgs Field. Scientists know from theoretical calculations that there is an entire ocean of Higgs particles permeating space, and therefore, science has begun the search for these hidden particles.

As I write this, scientists are conducting high-energy collisions in their giant atom smasher at CERN (Centre Europeene pour la Recherche Nuclaire) in Geneva, Switzerland. Also at Fermi Lab in Illinois the same experiment is underway. The prediction is that these experiments will provide solid evidence of the Higgs particles. This would be the scientific proof of hidden extra dimensions (!), and surely with this kind of scientific knowledge, it would open up our understanding of the universe in new ways that cannot be imagined.

The proof of extra dimension would most certainly transform the way we see our universe, but already there are some interesting theories of how it could be structured. One of them is called the Holographic Universe, which, according to van Lommel's theory, gives the holographic life-review its information. The idea of a holographic universe is not new since the idea is taken from Plato's shadow world in his cave allegory. This theory suggests that our physical world, which we perceive to have three space dimensions, could instead be 'written' on a two dimensional surface, as a hologram.

What is interesting about the hologram theory is the way a hologram works. In the same way that every small part of a hologram contains the image of the whole, so too, does every part of the universe enfold the entire universe as a whole. Greene explains that,

> What we experience in the "volume" of the universe—in the bulk, as physicists often call it—would be determined by what takes place on the bounding surface, much as what we see in a holographic projection is determined by information encoded on a bounding piece of plastic.[43]

If we interpreted this bounding surface as the Platonic world, or spiritual world, which through encoded information, such as DNA, determines our physical world through its holographic projection, then I find this theory extremely interesting. In more, consciousness could very well be the source of the encoded information that determines what takes place in the physical world, working as a bridge between the material and immaterial dimensions--connecting all of the eleven dimensions.

Qualia Physics

As we have seen, science is rapidly evolving towards the edge of space and time. This is often referred to as "the end of time" or "the Singularity." In this search, science is also approaching what is believed to be a unified theory that explains everything.

Scientist Julian Barbour, in his book *The End of Time*, says that, "There are no laws of nature, just one law of the universe...the *universal equation*."[44] This is the search for an objective ultimate reality as the structure of our universe, and Barbour tells us further that,

> Such a framework, if realized, would show that space, time, and, by association, dimension are not essential defining elements of the universe. Rather, they are convenient notions that emerge from a more basic, atavistic, and primary state.[45]

I like his words "convenient notions," that emerge from a more basic and fundamental level of reality. Our physical world, including our laws of physics and our sense data, are those convenient notions. Thereby matter is not the essential defining element of our universe, but there is something else—a larger picture—which is what the out-of-dimension experience tells us.

With the advance of new science it is pretty clear that we are moving in this direction in our understanding of the universe. The wave-particle duality was proven almost a century ago, and so, it is time to begin to make new conclusions in the dawn of this new reality.

If we accept that it is possible that out-of-dimension experiencers have been in contact with this ultimate reality, then we must ask ourselves what we can learn from their accounts. Can it be that these people are not all 'love sick,' and do in fact experience *love* as the nature of this ultimate structure? And could it be, then, that the view of Darwinism, is too cold in this light?

To me, it seems very clear that the worldview of Darwinism is out of date. How can we kill other humans in cold numbers when our universe is interconnected? Quantum entanglement raises an important question about interconnectedness—what does it mean that everything is connected? And this question leads us to the next question: What is the *quality* of our connection with each other and the world?

Science investigates the *what* and the *how* of natural phenomena 'objectively.' In other words, science only deals with the physical world, which now seems to be no more than a convenient notion of reality. But it leaves out the question of morality and the experience of being alive, what in philosophy is called *qualia*.

This is the idea that experience is fundamental and precedes anything else, which means that qualia is a kind of proto-conscious experience that exists at the ultimate level of the universe. Again this is a lot like what some near-death experiences give evidence to—that the true nature of reality is pure conscious experience.

Professor Stuart Hameroff, M.D., at the Center of Consciousness Studies in Arizona has what I believe to be one of the most cutting edge scientific theories. After working with Roger Penrose on a theory of the origin of consciousness, he has taken the Platonic values even further. He explains that if the Platonic values; mathematical truth, aesthetics, ethics *and experience* do exist, then, a place to look would be at the most fundamental level of reality.[46]

This way of thinking is not far from the aetherlike entity, or divine spirit and other scientist have pursued it before. In the 18th century, Leibniz described the universe as infinite fundamental units (monads) as a psychological being. Later Whitehead described monads as mind-like entities as "occasions of experiences" with a quality of "feeling." And recently, Wheeler and Charlmers told us that the fundamental reality includes "experiential aspects" leading to consciousness.[47]

Having had a powerful out-of-dimension experience, I find these scientific theories very interesting. To me, it seems very likely that the experience of this fundamental reality is the experience of truth, since the fundamental level of reality must be the true nature of reality. Hameroff suggests this possibility by saying that, "The Planck scale [fundamental level] is all there is...if qualia are fundamental and exists at the Planck scale, then why not Platonic values like truth and beauty, (good and evil)."[48]

He then asks the very important question: Whether truth could not be ingrained in the most basic level of reality. Could morality, which seems relative and abstract to us, "simply exist in the empty space of the universe?"[49] I find this question extremely interesting and even more important in the times we live in. Social Darwinism has told us that morality is relative, and we have a new religion called science that totally leaves out this aspect of life.

I grew up thinking like this that truth was relative, but then when I left my body I experienced something beyond this belief, something so overwhelmingly true that I was left in total awe. In our materialistic worldview everything we do not see is empty. Our endless universe, besides the stars, looks black and empty, but science reveals that nothing is empty—not even space is empty.

In quantum physics this emptiness is called the *quantum vacuum*, but it is not empty. N.C. Panda tells us that,

> According to the quantum theory, "emptiness" means "the absence of all particles"; but it does not mean "space which contains nothing" or "space which is nothing". Even a perfect vacuum is filled with forces and fields. Neither is a vacuum associated with inactivity.[50]

The invisible higher dimensional space is made of wave-fields that are interconnected. And this dimension is not only made of energy—it also contains information. Hameroff lets us know that, "The amount of information at the Planck scale is absolutely mind-boggling,"[51] and again referencing the out-of-dimension experience this would make sense, because the ultimate reality is beyond comprehension. Thereby, both the amount of information and the intensity of the energy would relate this to the out-of-dimension experience.

Physicist David Bohm uses the name "the implicate order of being"[52] and for me, this truly describes the near-death experience. The out-of-dimension experience leaves this dimension and enters the implicate order of being to reveal that this order of being is love. One experiencer explains this very clearly: "The Light told me everything was Love, and I mean everything!"[53] This was also my experience of the nature of the implicate order of being.

Of course, this is a subjective experience, but when science rejects subjective experience it at the same time runs into a contradiction. At the fundamental level of the universe, objective observation becomes impossible through what is called "objective reduction." The closer science gets to the truth the less objective it becomes and so science is faced with a paradox—its objectively-based model of truth dissolves into subjectivity. The observer becomes part of the experiment and affects the outcome of what should have been an objective result, and thereby, as van Lommel explains, at this fundamental level of the universe, "only subjectivity remains."[54]

Near-death researcher Bruce Greyson makes a conclusion that describes the problem that science is facing:

> I think that there is something more than what our simplistic models tell us. I am a scientist and I don't think that it is something

that science can't ever address, but I think that science is going to have to grow with it before we can really get a grasp on this...I know that something is missing for our models.[55]

Definitely there is something missing since we only can account for about 96 percent of the universe we live in, whereby we are only scratching the surface, or as Tiller said, we are only perceiving a small part of reality. Van Lommel believes that the missing link in science is subjectivity, and therefore, he says that, "subjectivity has to be included in science."[56]

The message from the out-of-dimension experience tells us that this missing piece is love, and brave cutting edge scientists come to this same conclusion: Morality exists in the fabric of 'empty' space. Or as Tiller has said, not only is morality ingrained in the fabric of the universe, but, "Love is the creative force" in our universe.[57]

For me, it would seem very probable that this information at the fundamental level of the universe has been "programmed" with love. If the source of this information is an "architect," then love would seem to be is part of the design of life. As regards to strict materialism and Darwinism, I will let Einstein finish this chapter:

"Subtle is the Lord, malicious He is not."[58]

PART II

AWAKENING

Chapter Six

Who Am I?

In ancient Greece at the time of the birth of Western civilization, there was a center, a place of wisdom. This place was the oracle in Delphi, which was the place where people came to seek insight and guidance. Upon the oracle was written "Know Thyself;" to know yourself was regarded as the most important insight—the height of wisdom.

The old Greeks asked the same question that Rene Descartes asked again more than two thousand years later: Who am I? To know who you are is to know your true self, and as Descartes wanted to point to the essence of our being, so did the Greeks, desiring to guide the way to this same center of our existence.

Consciousness—to be aware—is the first state of being. It is our first experience and that which exists before anything else. It is the core of our existence, and the essence of our being. Knowing this center of our being is thereby the meaning center of existence. This the Greeks understood, and their most holy place was dedicated to answering this question.

This is also what we found in the Bible before, where God said to Moses: "I AM WHO AM."[1] Thereby, God is "HE WHO IS" or "*being* itself,"[2] which is the answer to the question. God is the center of being—the essence of existence. And with the highest wisdom telling us to know ourselves—the question; who am I becomes the key in our search for Truth and the nature of God.

Consciousness

Our last chapter, which centered on science, has prepared the way for the empirical approach to identity through the study of consciousness. Science tells us that the universe is made of energy, but information is just as important an ingredient. We can see this in the case of DNA, which is the genetic information of life, and without which there could be no life. The big question in science about DNA is where this information comes from—what is the origin of biological information?

Classical science is having great trouble answering this question. It has been said that human DNA contains more organized information than the entire Encyclopedia Britannica. Even Bill Gates has been humble enough to explain just how complicated it is: "DNA is like a software program, only much more complex than anything we've ever devised."[3]

The problem that classical science faces is that it claims that something came out of nothing, which is logically impossible. This something out of nothing is similar to the Bible where God creates the world in seven days, also out of nothing. N. C. Panda, makes the joking remark about this classical view, and says that, "Science, being materialistic, rejected the Creator, but did not abandon the concept of creation out of nothing."[4] As God said, "Let there be light," so Darwinists said, "Let there be consciousness."

Darwinism claims that consciousness evolved out of biology— something unconscious developed consciousness—but the problem is that classical science cannot account for what produces consciousness. In *The Case for a Creator*, Lee Strobel quotes Colin McGinn asking the question in a very humorous way: "How did evolution convert the water of biological tissue into the wine of consciousness?"[5]

On other issues, such as the big bang, scientists do not seem to disagree; the big bang could not have come out of nothing—something must have been before. From my experience of a non-material reality outside the body, it seems very clear that science, and especially classical science needs to catch up on the question of consciousness. It seems that pure consciousness does exist 'out there' beyond the body in another dimension, and with almost 96 percent of the universe being unknown to us, there is really something for science to investigate.

Consciousness studies are a fairly new field within science, even though we can go far back to Descartes' conviction that the body and mind are separate. In *Infinite Mind*, Dr. Valerie Hunt explains that early in the last century, neurologist Sir Arthur Sherrington did not believe that the body and mind were one. Then later, Karl Pribram received a Nobel Prize for his brain hologram research, where he pointed to that the holographic images that we see in our mind, were in fact existing outside the brain.[6]

More recently, contemporary neurosurgeon Wilder Penfield discovered that the anaesthetized mind continued to work even thought the brain was inactive: "Brain waves were found to be nearly absent while the mind was just as active as it was in normal states."[7] Penfield concluded that, "it is the mind which experiences and it is the brain which records the experience."[8] He, as well as many scientists, was unable to find the mind's energy source within the brain, and therefore, he concluded that the mind is primary to thought. He also believed that the mind *is* the stream of consciousness.[9]

Valerie Hunt sums up in her book that mind cannot be explained in a material framework because "the mind is more a field reality, a quantum reality."[10] This leads us into quantum theory and the new studies on consciousness. Basically, as we saw, the science predicts that space is not empty, but the fundamental level of the universe, or the vacuum, is full of consciousness as a quantum field of energy.

This is not a new idea, since we can also find in ancient Hindu religion that the source of the manifested universe is Brahman—pure consciousness. As this idea is part of religion and the mystical experience, it is also part of the near-death experience where some people, including myself, experience a state of pure consciousness.

Also as we went through earlier, in Buddhism we find that the fundamental reality is called Buddha nature, or clear light nature. The clear light of the ultimate reality is similar to the core experience of the near-death experience of meeting the light. In this experience there seems to be no distinction between the light and the mind, and it has been directly suggested that the light and mind *are one*, or the mind is a matrix for the light.[11]

Here again I find Dr. Stuart Hameroff very interesting as he attempts to explain, from a scientific viewpoint, how the out-of-dimension and near-death experience is possible. He suggests that,

> Let's say consciousness already occurs at the Planck scale [fundamental level], and is connected to our brains by quantum interactions. Let's say the brain stops working, but the quantum information is still present. Maybe that information could leak out into space-time, outside the brain.[12]

This would be a theory on how it is possible for the mind to leave the body in the out-of-dimension experience. Consciousness is in and around everything in the universe, and therefore, it can both be experienced inside and outside the brain.

Hameroff sums this up in the following manner:

> Consciousness is a self-organizing process at this fundamental level of the universe—we *are* really the universe. We are a process occurring at this basic level. So we are connected to the universe, and we are also connected to each other, because the universe has this property of non-locality; everything is connected to everything. So it's a kind of spiritual thing because basically we are the fundamental level of the universe.[13]

Consciousness is the ground of being and that makes us, when we are conscious, the fundamental level of the universe. We are *that* which is—being itself. This scientific theory makes a lot of sense to me, because it directly describes my experience. I experienced my true nature as pure and absolute consciousness, exactly as if the essence of my being was the true nature of reality. I believe that the near-death research is an important piece of evidence that points in the direction of this new science.

One near-death account comes very close to describing exactly this point: "It totally absorbed my consciousness. It seemed to radiate from the very center of the consciousness I was in and to shine out in every direction through the infinite expanses of the universe."[14]

Another scientist, Amit Goswami, concludes the same: "The universe is self-aware, but it is self-aware through us. We are the meaning of the universe. We are not the geographical center of the universe—Copernicus was right about that—but we are the meaning center of the universe."[15]

If this is so, then, how do we experience the meaning center of the universe—our true nature? To experience the center of our being, we need to go beyond the brain—beyond the world that is defined by our senses. This means that we need to go beyond the material world, which is why it is so difficult for science.

Dr. Andrew Newberg, author of *The Mystical Mind* and professor at the University of Pennsylvania Medical Center, explains that,

> There is no real way to get outside of the brain, and in some senses, we have to have the brain get out of its own way, in order to see what is really out there. And since we can't do that, at least from a scientific perspective, we have to turn to a more experiential perspective.[16]

Western Enlightenment

Not knowing who we are—having an identity crisis—was called "homelessness" by philosopher Martin Heidegger. In his *Letter on Humanism*, shortly after the Second World War, he said that, "Homelessness is coming to be the destiny of the world."[17] After experiencing two world wars, it is easy to understand his inability to "locate man within being," as regard to being human. He explained that to be human can be understood as that "in which the essence of man preserves the source that determines him."[18]

Being, in its essence, is already illuminated by truth, which cannot be said about the creation of concepts and ism's. If we are to find truth, we need to look into our essence and the light that preserves us as the source of our identity. This light is the light in enlightenment, and it is by this light that we find who we are, our home and true identity.

As we saw in the chapter on religion, the God of the *Roman* Catholic Church did not want Adam to eat the fruit of the Three of Knowledge. To the ancient Greeks, the Gnostics, and the Eastern world, this would seem suspicious: What sort of God is this? Unless Adam was completely untrustworthy there would be no reason to withhold the truth from him, since this would lead to his destruction. To the Gnostics self-ignorance is "a form of self-destruction," because "whoever remains ignorant, a creature of oblivion, cannot experience fulfillment."[19]

History showed that not only Adam was untrustworthy, so too was the God of the Church. The atrocities committed by the 'only true church' by authority of this jealous God are unparalleled in history, even to the Roman Empire itself. This was why Luther reformed the Church.

The reformation was the beginning of the *Age of Enlightenment*, not only because Adam was now free from control, but also because he was now able to read the Bible himself, which Luther had translated. By being able to read for himself, Adam could now eat the fruits from the Three of Knowledge and begin to see for himself.

Descartes' *Meditations* in the 17th century was also a tree of knowledge. Descartes freed the individual from the outside authority, and moved the source of truth back within man. First he said that he would "attack straightaway those principles which supported everything I once believed."[20] Then he pointed to the light of nature (intuition), and he said when we see clear and distinct ideas in this light, we "need not assign to those ideas an author distinct" from ourselves.[21]

The important point here in history was that Descartes moved our source of truth from the outside authority, the God of the Church, to the inside authority of our own essence. At that time, saying that the truth is within, transformed people from suppressed victims into free individuals with the freedom to choose. Even though today there are also other powers that are trying to control us, this point is the same that others cannot tell us who we are or how we should live.

Then in 1784, Immanuel Kant asked the pressing question, "What is Enlightenment?" His answer was that enlightenment was our relationship with ourselves—how we relate to ourselves. This relationship happens in our mind and is defined by the way we relate to the present moment. Often we bring our personal history from the past into the present, and thereby we see things dimly because we relate our present experience to past experiences. To see things clearly we need to have a liberated relationship with the past, which then gives us a free access to the present. The enlightened position of the mind is one where we are free of the burden of the past. With this position of detached freedom, we can act freely in the present moment.

To help us get free of the burden of the past, today we use therapy. Personally, I have gained great insight through the use of therapy and psychoanalysis. Carl G. Jung said that, "The supreme aim of the *opus psychologicum* is conscious realization, and the first step is to make oneself conscious of contents that have hitherto been projected."[22] He also told us that this journey leads to "self-knowledge," and thereby to "the distinction between what one really is and what is projected into one, or what one imagines oneself to be."[23]

There is a very important connection between our true nature and enlightenment—our true self is enlightened. And as Jung explained, to have self-knowledge, we need to know what is being projected in our mind and what we are imagining. Another contemporary thinker in the field of sociology, Zygmunt Bauman, talks about the difference between *having* an identity and *making* an identity.[24] Here having an identity is founded on who we are—our true nature, whereas making an identity is what Jung talks about: projecting or imagining an identity.

In today's complex world many forces are competing for control of our minds, and therefore, having an identity can sometimes seem more difficult than letting this world make us one through conditioning. The Gnostics explained that without having an identity a person is "being driven by impulses he does not understand,"[25] and this is what happens when we let other people, or the world around us, make our identity for us.

This is the relationship between our subjective experience of ourselves and the way we experience the world 'outside.' Inspired by Sartre's essay on stickiness, Mary Douglas in *Purity and Danger* explains that what makes our identity is a slime that sticks to our true identity. The slime that makes our identity possesses us by crossing the boundary between our identity and it:

> When I believe that I possess it, behold by a curious reversal, it possesses me...If an object which I hold in my hands is solid, I can let go when I please; its inertia symbolizes for me my total power... Yet here is the slimy reversing the terms; (my self) is suddenly *compromised*, I open my hands, I want to let go of the slimy and it sticks to me, if draws me , it sucks me...I am no longer the master... The slime is like a liquid seen in a nightmare, when all its properties are animated by a sort of life and turn back against me.[26]

What makes the slime stick is what in the East would be called attachment. It is by attachment to projections and imagination that we create an identity that is not our true identity. This is how we experience an identity crisis when we finally have made ourselves an identity that subsumes our true identity.

The way out of this crisis is to know our true identity and hold on to it. Recognize your identity and do not let the slime stick to it: "If I dive into the water, if I plunge into it, if I let myself sink in it, I experience no discomfort, for I do not have any fear whatsoever that I may dissolve in it; I remain a solid in its liquidity."[27]

Eastern Enlightenment

The East holds the longest tradition of enlightenment and in going beyond the brain. Here teachings on enlightenment have been passed on for thousands of years. The Bhagavadagita explains about enlightenment, and building on this tradition, the Buddha is known as the greatest teacher of enlightenment of all time. In Buddhism, enlightenment can be explained as the liberation from our thoughts. Instead of being our thoughts, we shift perspective to watching our thought—we are observing our thoughts without identifying with our thoughts.

Enlightenment is the liberation from thought identification to thought observation, and this is what it means for the brain to get out of its own way. Beyond the brain and its thoughts we experience that we are still there, and this experience is liberation—the experience of our true nature.

To explain this, a mirror is often used as a metaphor for the mind, or consciousness. Our mind is an empty mirror in which thoughts occur as reflections. We are the mirror. Our thoughts, as reflections in the mirror, are our subjective self, or ego. By observing our thoughts we can see that these reflections come and go in the mirror, but when we watch closely we find something behind these reflections that is clear and stable. This is the mirror—our true nature.

Knowing our true identity, we can observe the reflections as they change from pleasant to unpleasant thoughts and back again, but since we no longer identify with the reflections we have now become liberated from them. This simply means that we are no longer controlled by our thoughts.

We now control our thoughts, and can select positive and happy thoughts, instead of negative and unhappy thoughts. This is enlightenment and freedom from our thoughts, which leads us to the essence of our nature. This was what the Buddha taught, and all his 84,000 teachings can all be condensed into one line: Recognize your essence.[28]

As we learn to control our mind and practice mindfulness, we discover our true identity more and more fully. We find that our true nature is positive and loving as the mirror is clear and bright. The Buddhists say that the mirror is empty—not in the Western understanding of nothingness, but empty of thoughts. As quantum physics tell us that space is full of energy, so too, is the true nature of the mind full of unborn and unlimited possibility. We could call this unborn and un-manifested reality quantum superposition in which everything is possible.

A movie projector is also used as a metaphor for the empty mind. The empty mind is the light of the projector in which the film (our thoughts) is projected. In other words the empty mind projects awareness onto the thoughts within our mind. By going really deep within the mind, we can discover that all we truly are is the clear light of the projector, and we can observe that the film is not created by us, but by the outside world as reflections in our mirror. Thereby, we can see how all the reflections are really impersonal—the only thing personal is the light behind the reflections. The reflections are karmic patterns in the world outside, but here inside, we are free to see beyond this game of life and let the light of our mind shine through it all.

To arrive at this realization, meditation is used as a tool to calm the mind. It is clear that in a hectic and busy day, it is all too easy to get caught up in the game of life. For our Western mind that operates by logic and is always busy analyzing, meditation can seem quite foreign. Personally, I know this to sometimes be a problem. But what is even a bigger problem for our Western mind is our either/or logic. This thinking in black and white, which constantly seeks the negation, can be a damaging element in critical rationalism. Most of us know (or try to escape) people who are always negative and always criticizing. These are not bad people; they are simply prisoners of our Western black and white logic that constantly seeks the negation.

The Buddhist tradition tells us that negation lacks the oneness with the parts, and therefore, we should abandon "the poison of contradictions." Being able to discriminate is an important function of the mind, but a dualistic mind ruled by negation is not a happy mind because it is disconnected from its own true nature. Our true identity is beyond conceptual thinking, and it is by redrawing this conceptualization that we can experience the true nature of the mind.

This is a very subtle process of the mind as the energy vibration of our true nature is extremely soft. One way to experience the subtlety of this energy is through conversation. By following the flow of energy in a conversation, we can learn a lot about the subtlety of our mind. We can see that to be completely clear and open in the mind requires considerable effort. The slightest aversion or attachment changes the energy of a conversation instantaneously. By observing the causes of the changes in the flow of energy, we can see our unconscious patterns of behavior. And if we look even closer by being very mindful, we can see that the energy actually speaks. We can read the energy of other people as they can read the energy we send out. The energy does not lie—it speaks the Truth—about our intensions and who we really are.

Thus, by being fully present we can see the true nature of other people, while being mindful of ourselves and what we reflect on to the world. This can then transform our own interaction with the world towards being more truthful, while at the same time help us to see the true nature of others. Underneath the manifested reality beyond the patterns of behavior, we can see the eternal and true nature of all of humanity. By holding on to the true nature of ourselves and others we can see the lie without becoming the lie. This is the element of enlightenment that transforms our world by letting in the light from the true nature of reality.

To calm and fine-tune the mind to these subtle energies, Buddhism uses meditation to practice mindfulness and reach enlightenment. Meditation is basically a technique of stilling the mind's "business" to reach a mindful or empty state. Many people are mindful naturally, while others have never had the experience of the true nature of mind. If you have not experienced meditation and feel that you would like to be more mindful, then I highly recommend meditation. There are many places to do meditation, and for me, the deepest and best meditation is experienced through Vippassana meditation. This is usually a ten day retreat of silent meditation that helps you go very deep within the mind and clear many layers of confusion.

To explain how meditation works, I will briefly explain the three steps in the meditation practice that I personally use. The first step is to sit comfortably in a silent room with the back straight and upright. You close your eyes and begin to calm the mind. To help calm the mind, you can focus on your breathing: in, out, in, out, etc. In the first step as you try to calm the mind, you will experience that your thoughts are many and random.

In the second step, as your mind calms, you will notice the thoughts starting to slow down. You can observe a thought coming into your mind, and then leaving again. This is perfectly all right. The practice of the second step is to not feed the thoughts energy. If a thought arises and you feed it energy by going into the thought, this thought will take you away from your center, just as a simple thought of a small thing can run far away with you. When you stop feeding your thoughts energy, you will experience that they come and go while you are still there. This is the essential part of the second step—the change from being your thoughts to observing your thoughts. This is also the liberating step in meditation where you gain control of your own mind through being mindful.

In the third step, you now become a witness to your thoughts by observing them instead of entering them. At this stage you will find that when you stop feeding the thoughts energy, they will slow down and your mind begins to become still. By going deep into the stillness you can also see how your thoughts completely stop and you will have the experience that time stops as well. This is deep meditation and what the Buddhists call the experience of emptiness. The self you experience when the mind is empty of thoughts is your true nature.

Step three reveals to us our true and enlightened nature, and through the practice of meditation this can serve as our rock foundation. However, even though we cannot, or do not always, arrive at the third step—step two is enough to help us in our personal transformation. Through mindfulness and being able to observe our thoughts, we can see what some Buddhists call "the hook," which we bite when we let ourselves fall into our negative patterns.

Through the mindful observation of the root cause that makes us fall into patterns, we make the subconscious conscious. The subconscious is also connected to our feelings, since besides being controlled by the way we think, as animals we are also controlled by the way we feel. Probably the biggest misconception about Buddhism is that we are not supposed to feel at all. The aim is only to control our negative emotions that cause negative actions and bad karma.

It is really about who is in the driver's seat of your life: you, or the negative patterns of your past. When we are in control of ourselves and this identity is based on our true nature, then we can cultivate positive actions and good karma. In the large context, it is really about not adding to the negative karma already in the world. I believe that when we look at the amount of conflict and war in our world, then surely we need to tame this anger. As a man, I know this is an important step in our evolution.

This is why the Buddha also thought our actions are connected to our sensations. The mind and body are deeply connected as our biology affects our mind and vice versa. The free mind comes from taking control over our biology so that the mind controls the body instead of the body controlling the mind—the body becomes servant of the mind.

To see how the two interact and affect each other is the key to transforming our negative behavior because biology is at the root of our actions. Many of our actions start as a *reaction* to a sensation, either pleasant or unpleasant. When we experience something pleasant we have a pleasant sensation; when we experience something unpleasant, we have an unpleasant sensation. These sensations turn into either craving or aversion, as a reaction to pleasant and unpleasant. When we recognize that the body has a memory, then we realize that we are now actually at the root of our patterns.

Sometimes we are not aware of our reactions—why we react the way we do. Childhood experiences and conditioning are part of our subconscious behavioral patterns. Take fear as an example. If we observe our body reactions during the fear-inducing event, we can see that the fear is connected to a sensation. If we in this moment become aware of the sensation, and remember that we are the mirror and not the images reflected in it, then we can stay mindful without reacting to the sensation. We can now start to liberate ourselves from this pattern of fear by being mindful of the body's sensation of fear without reaction to it in the mind.

Anger works the same way. It starts with a tense or unpleasant body sensation and then angry thoughts arise. If we become aware of the sensation before it turns into anger, then we can start to change our reaction to it and our consciousness will evolve as we grow out of our negative patterns. By becoming conscious of our subconscious patterns of behavior, we can break the chain at its root level and start to transform ourselves and the world around us.

This is how, through mindfulness, we can begin to see the world as it really is beyond patterns and illusions. By being mindful of our true nature we can stop the karmic inflation of reality and begin to see what is actually there. The true nature of mind becomes the rock upon which we see through the false concepts of the mind. Thereby, we arrive at the *right view* on reality and this right view becomes the foundation of our *right actions*.

Karmic patterns are not part of our true nature—they are part of the manifest world. To be real and to experience who we are, we need to move beyond into the un-manifest and unlimited world of our true nature. Just the same, when we die and leave the body, we also leave this karmic world of delusion to enter the ultimate nature of reality.

The true nature of mind is the door through which we enter into the ultimate reality of existence. The Buddhists teach us that to leave the karmic world behind; we cannot be attached to it. Non-attachment is a mind in equilibrium without craving or aversion. Again, non-attachment is not the nihilistic perception of nothingness, but the abandoning of conceptual thinking, which leaves the mind calm to experience itself. The true nature of the mind is naturally full of light and unlimited love. This is very similar to the experience of the light in the near-death experience. In fact, "The light experienced in meditation has many of the qualities of the light of the NDE."[29]

Buddhism teaches that when we die, we encounter this light—the Luminous Bardo of Dharmata, Dharmata meaning true nature and luminosity referring to the light that is naturally present.[30] As the near-death experience gives evidence to, this ultimate reality is beyond our human understanding, and in Buddhism it is bright and unimaginably positive. Since Buddhism has the most in-depth explanation of how we enter this light, in the next chapter I will use the Buddhist insights as a guide to leaving the body when we die.

Chapter Seven

Leaving the Body

I have called this chapter Leaving the Body, even though it is about what we call death. This I have done to underscore the importance of seeing death from a new perspective—not as an entry into nothingness—but as a door into another dimension.

Death in the modern world has been called the scandal of reason,[1] because reason is unable to overcome the paradox of death. In its objection to faith, reason refuses to face this paradox by trying to understand death. By rejecting the afterlife as unreasonable, death is made a journey into the unknown. Most of us go to great lengths to leave home for even a week of travel, yet our modern society does nothing to prepare us for the great journey into death.

The Pope has explained that we are being deprived of the truth of existence, and therefore, we will suffer great loss: "The West has long been endangered by this aversion to the questions that underlie its rationality, and can only suffer great harm thereby."[2]

Through its inability to understand and thus deal with death, the modern mindset has made death meaningless. In my native country, I read an article about death by a highly recognized doctor who is a member of The Ethical Council of Denmark. He used the Greek philosopher, Epicurus, to make his point. "Death is not to be feared—when it is there, I am not—and when I am there, it is not."[3]

Epicurus was a strict materialist who said that "pleasure is happiness,"[4] and even though his thinking is more than two thousand years old, his view fits with today's modern rationalistic worldview. With reason's failure to overcome the paradox of death, we are left with modern technology's sometimes extreme ways of overcoming the causes of death. Not wanting to touch on the subject of death, all resources are focused on overcoming the causes of death. It seems that since reason is unable to understand death, we focus our efforts on trying to defeat that which we fear.

These have been my personal observations from working as a volunteer visiting dying cancer patients. Our modern world does everything possible to defend its people while alive, but when death is inevitable, people are left to fight this last battle alone. Having separated death from life, life is missing its other half. Without an understanding of the meaning of death, we cannot understand the meaning of life.

Death

Death is difficult. Leaving loved ones behind, or bearing the loss of loved ones, is the heaviest part of life. Going through a painful death, or being the witness to the pain of a loved one dying, is almost unbearable. When my father died I was in shock, feeling as if I had been hit by a train. The pain was so heavy to bear that it choked me and scared me at first. However, what helped me out of this wreckage was to accept and get in touch with the pain.

I took a full week off preparing the funeral and during this time I went through all of my father's things with all the memories connected to them. For a full week I cried, culminating in the speech that I gave at the funeral. This speech contained the most difficult words I have ever spoken. But just after the funeral I felt something lift and the next day I began to feel the pain leave my heart. It was as if during that whole week I was able to take it all in and let it all out.

In *Perfect Endings*, Robert Sachs says: "No death is good. No death is bad. Death just is." Death is a natural part of life, and Sachs explains that whatever form death takes, it is still the perfect conclusion to the life that we have lived.[5] No matter the kind of death we experience, it is still something we must come to terms with through acceptance.

After having accepted the death of my father, I found that the only thing I regretted was the things that I did not have time to say before he died—the things left unsaid, like "I love you." Now, this chance was lost, and all of a sudden, I wanted to say this more than anything in the world.

Death is an absolute, and therefore, it makes life extremely important. What is said and done before has profound meaning, and it is almost as if death sometimes can teach us the meaning of life. What we have done with our lives becomes the teaching tool in the school of life. The fact that many people experience a life-review on the other side, strongly suggests that life lessons are a very important part of dying. Peter Fenwick tells us that, "The life review seems to give an absolution, something which may be psychologically very necessary at the end of a life."[6]

In the same way, learning on this side of the dying process is equally important. Sachs explains that to have a perfect ending to life can be summed up in one phrase: *Pay Attention.*

> Pay attention not only to the present but also by reflecting on the days, weeks, months, and perhaps years that have brought you to this moment...You are learning constantly. Life's school is never out until the final bell...For no matter what we conceive of happening afterward—heaven, hell, another life—we continue to work through a labyrinth that is deep, often incomprehensible, yet workable and in keeping with our original design.[7]

Sachs' final advice is: "Just relax. Pay attention. Suspend judgment. Opportunity abounds. *Remember: Nothing is ever lost.*"[8] For me, after having gone through the pain, I realized that my father was not really gone. The love we shared—the energy of this love—was always there with me. When ever I would connect to this energy—my father would be there. In this way, I learned that love is never lost.

The near-death experience also testifies that nothing is ever lost. The final bell is but the doorbell of an unimaginable magnificent bright state of being on the other side. In my view, the research into the near-death experience is the best and most creditable good news of what is on the other side of this door. The news is so good that it should bring about a positive perspective with both the dying person and the loved ones.

One near-death account tells us that there is no reason for us or the person dying to fear death: "Before my experience I had wondered, like most, about death, and, like most, was afraid of the unknown. I now know that there is no pain, there is nothing other than the ending of one chapter and the turning of the page."[9]

Death is the beginning of a wonderful experience as we turn the page: "At 11.30 p.m. he stirred and said he had died. I asked him what it was like; he relied, 'Ecstasy'...'If anyone asks if there is a God I shall say yes, I have seen him'."[10] Another person reveals that, "My experience of death was wonderful. I was floating high up, no pain, great joy, and no fear...I was overwhelmed with joy."[11]

On the other side there is no pain anymore, even if the dying process is painful itself, we are liberated from this pain. One account explains: "The pain was replaced by this wonderful feeling, such a contrast to the pain and suffering...I would like to encourage people to be unafraid of death."[12] The light on the other side is so unbelievably wonderful that all pain experienced in this world completely disappears.

As a loved one witnessing the painful death of a person, I believe these testimonies can offer great comfort by understanding that the light on the other side is all good—all love. What was pain will be no more, and as the dying person, the light gives great hope and meaning to death. Knowing that this is where we go when we die can make us relax and concentrate on leaving this world in the best manner.

One account testifies that, "All my will was concentrated on 'going'. I never once thought of my husband or my children, who were quite young then. It all seemed terribly personal, nothing to do with anyone else."[13] The dying process is extremely personal on the other side, and knowing this can make us let go easier.

In *90 Minutes in Heaven*, Don Piper explains that,

> It was perfect, and I knew I had no needs and never would again. I didn't even think of earth or those left behind...My feelings have been that once we're actually in God's presence, we will never return to earth again, because it will be empty and meaningless by comparison.[14]

Outer Dissolution

The Tibetan Book of the Dead has the most comprehensive step-by-step description of the dying process of both the body and the mind. The process of the dying body is called *outer dissolution*, and this ancient description is being use in today's hospice work as a guide for the dying.

The text reveals how the elements of our body dissolve and how this is felt through our senses. According to Buddhism and Eastern religion, our body is made up of the five elements: earth, water, fire, air, and space. As each element dissolve there is a sense-experience to go with it: "The five inner elements of flesh, blood, body heat, space, and consciousness are dependent on the five outer elements of earth, water, fire, wind, and sky. At the time of death, the five inner elements gradually dissolve into one another."[15]

The stages of dissolution happen in the following order:

The earth element, which corresponds to the flesh of the body, dissolves into water. At this time the body becomes very heavy and we feel as though we cannot move. The water element, which corresponds to the blood of the body, dissolves into fire or heat. At this time we feel very dry because the water in the body is evaporating...The fire element, which corresponds to body heat, dissolves into air or breath. At this time the heat leaves the body and we feel cold. The wind or air element, which corresponds to space, dissolves into consciousness. At this time we can no longer inhale or exhale; we can no longer breathe.[16]

When first earth dissolves into water, the experience is weakening as the body is melting. Visual acuity deteriorates and everything seems like a mirage of water. Then water dissolves into fire and the fluids of the body dry out with the sensation of becoming numb. With this numbness, auditory acuity goes away, one can no longer hear well, and there is a sensation of being surrounded by smoke.

Then fire dissolves into wind. Inhalation weakens and the sense of smell goes away. One feels cold and surrounded by a burst of sparks. Then wind dissolves into space, and breathing stops. This is where gross consciousness dissolves, and it is the end of the gross mind-body experience.[17]

The connection between the mind and the dissolution of the elements is deep and profound, since the elements are created from mind. In Soygal Rinpoche's book *The Tibetan Book of Living and Dying*, Kalu Rinpoche reveals that, "It is from mind, which embodies the five elemental qualities, that the physical body develops."[18] This means that as the body dissolves into the mind, this is where we feel the sensations of this dissolution, and so, this is the biggest part of dying—the inner dissolution.

Inner Dissolution

The dissolution of the body is followed by an *inner dissolution* that dissolves the gross mind-body experience. The inner dissolution of the mind is from the gross to the subtle, where the gross mind of confusion is dissolved into the subtle mind of its own true nature. This dissolution is a powerful transformation of consciousness, which happens as the awareness that identifies with the elements that make up the body is transformed into an awareness of the true nature of the mind.

This transformation also includes the powerful experience of leaving the body. The experience of leaving our body is an unusual experience, and in the near-death experience Raymond Moody observes that many people describe being confused.[19] For me, it was an extremely powerful sensation as if I was free falling while my body was dissolving in an internal explosion. Leaving the body and meeting the light is an intensely emotional sensation that the near-death experiencer cannot find words to describe.[20]

This is when we discover that we have left our body. When the body is alive it is the support of our consciousness, but when we die the body is no longer able to support our consciousness. Therefore, leaving the body is described as the experience of falling, since there is no longer any feeling of weight connected to our consciousness.[21]

As our consciousness leaves the body, the gross mind is dissolved with the elements, and we find ourselves in the subtle mind of our true nature. The reality that we perceive through our senses is manifested by our senses, and these senses are made from the elements that make our body. The reason we see reality as it is in this physical dimension is that our senses are dependent on the elements that make them. When the elements dissolve, the senses and the awareness connected to the senses also dissolve and our mind awakens to a new reality.

This new reality dawns at the moment that the two elements meet—the gross mind and the subtle mind. The gross mind is the ground of confusion since it is connected to our senses and our relative world. But the subtle mind is the ground of liberation because the true nature of reality dawns from experiencing it.[22]

The gross mind, which we can also call the conceptual mind, gives birth to the enlightened mind; "What remains when all of these thought states have ceased, is simply the unconstructed nature of mind...it is the naked awareness itself."[23]

The Buddhist tradition calls this awakening to the naked awareness the meeting of mother and child. The mother is the clear light of naked awareness (emptiness), and "this is the fundamental, inherent nature of everything, which underlies our whole experience, and which manifests in its full glory at the moment of death."[24]

The naked mind and the clear light are one, as the true nature of our mind meets its mother as the ultimate reality. The naked awareness is both empty and luminous, which is the fundamental nature of everything. The naked mind and the clear light meet as "old friends," like a river flowing into the ocean. In this flowing into the ocean all that is left of the mind is space that is "totally free from mental constructs, yet naturally endowed with cognizant wakefulness."[25] And as the dissolution of the gross mind is over, we awaken as a mental body—a point of awareness.

The inner dissolution process has the following steps. First consciousness dissolves into space, and then space dissolves into luminosity. Then luminosity, or light, dissolves into union, which dissolves into wisdom. Wisdom then dissolves into spontaneous presence, which then finally dissolves into primordial purity.[26]

These experiences we also find in the near-death experience. Here among the core experiences we can find "illuminated environment" as luminosity, and "feelings of oneness" as union.[27] We also have "profound knowledge"[28] as wisdom, and "heightened awareness"[29] as spontaneous presence. At the point when the luminosity dissolves into union, in the Tibetan tradition, the essence of "peaceful deities" are experienced.[30] The experience of peace is also one of the most common core experiences in the near-death studies, which is experienced in some studies by up to 82 percent.[31]

Awakening

The experience of peace is a sensation that is extremely positive and filled with the experience of love and joy beyond imagination. There is a feeling of completeness and oneness that is truly out of this dimension. Fenwick tells us that,

> Not only is the experience felt as complete, but this completeness is a "coming home." It is as if they had always known this state and that birth, life with its pains, and death, are all a departure from an underlying consciousness.[32]

This experience of coming home is experienced as the ultimate truth of reality, exactly as Buddhism describes it to be the fundamental level of reality. Some near-death experiencers feel that they have "seen through the very texture of the universe into its ultimate structure."[33] One person describes: "I just knew, the light held all the answers,"[34] and another explains that "the meaning and purpose of life and the universe itself. I could not possibly know the answers but I did!"[35]

From Carl Jung we can learn that,

What happens after death is so unspeakably glorious that our imagination and our feelings do not suffice to form even an approximate conception of it...The dissolution of our time-bound form in eternity brings no loss of meaning.[36]

Plato calls this an entry into the sky from where the true heaven and the true earth can be seen in the "true light."[37] Everything seen in the true light is incredibly beautiful, and much brighter than what we perceive in this dimension. In this place in the sky, all abilities like sight, hearing, and understanding are pure and far superior to anything we know on earth.[38]

Plato also speaks of a wholeness or oneness that can be experienced from there. In this way the true meaning of life is first revealed at the moment of death when we look into the mirror. We now see everything in its true light and this is the whole point of Plato's message; it is first when we die that we discover the true purpose of life. This is also what the mirror of death reveals to us in Buddhism, and this is what the near-death experience tells us about the next dimension. It is first at the time of death, when we leave the body and enter the next dimension, that the true meaning of the universe is revealed to us.

Here we can also use Plato's story about the prisoners in the cave, who are watching shadows of reality. Our conceptual mind and our senses have us caught in the cave, watching only shadows of reality. These shadows are what we experience as the physical dimension, and when we leave this dimension, we are like the prisoners freed of our chains, liberated to see the world outside the cave. This fits with Moody's accounts that describe the homecoming of death as the "escape from jail."[39]

This is what happens when we leave the body; we are liberated from the chains of our physical senses and set free to see existence in its true light. Fenwick tells us that "this emotional state is primary and spreads into whatever imagery arises...the essence of each of these experiences was the 'feeling state'...which seems to me to shape and define the near-death experience."[40] He also explains that the "predominant quality" of the light "is that of bliss and universal love."[41]

There are really no words and nothing in this dimension that can explain this sensation. One near-death account tries to describe it this way:

I was convinced no living person could experience such joy. The only way I can explain it is think of the happiest moment of your life, and when you do, that happiest moment is awful pain compared to what you feel, and I will swear to that.[42]

The best words we have are: ecstasy, bliss, perfect joy, complete happiness, absolute perfection, bursting love, groundless emotion. Still, the true nature of reality is beyond words and beyond our comprehension, but what is certain is that the meeting with this ultimate reality brings about an awakening: "The common ground between cultures and between individuals is that the NDE seems to be an 'awakening' experience."[43]

One near-death experiencer testifies that it is the awakening to, "A LOVE so incredibly powerful and intensely deep that I was astounded and even in a state of shock as it went through me. I never knew such a LOVE existed."[44] This is the experience of total awe — an awe awakening to the true nature of reality being love.

My own thought when entering into this dimension was: Wow! I did not know! This was the experience of raw and absolute truth — there is Truth! And this truth is Love. The realization of this totally overwhelmed me. I did not know because I thought that there was no truth. The next dimension is so overpowering that it leaves us in total awe and absolute humility. The meeting with this new dimension is so powerful, that it makes us awaken in the greatest revelation: It is all love — pure and absolute love — the true nature and fundamental reality of life is love.

Chapter Eight

The Negative Life-Review

"Delusion is a Divine curse
that makes someone envious, conceited, malicious,
so that he doesn't know the evil he does
will strike him back.

If he could see his nothingness
and his deadly, festering wound,
pain would arise from looking within,
and that pain would save him."[1]

The first time I read these words by the great Sufi Rumi I cried with tears from deep within my heart. The words hit me directly where my near-death experience had taken me years before. This poem was a precise description of the negative life-review that I went through. In it, I had looked into my nothingness, my deadly festering wound, and this pain of looking within had saved me.

In meeting the light outside my body I experienced truth—absolute truth. There is Truth even though we choose not to believe so. If we have rejected truth in life, we will have to face it in death. There is no running away and nothing to hide behind, because life does not end. Raymond Moody explains that there is "no possibility whatsoever either of misunderstanding or lying to the light,"[2] and an account tells us that, "You cannot lie; you cannot cheat. Not *there* you can't."[3] This is the point, even though we can try to reject it—*there* is Truth.

I was an atheist and I did not believe that there was truth in the universe. But I was wrong. When I left my body and met the light, I experienced the full power of this truth. This left me in total and all-overpowering awe: I did not know—it is all love! Not having known this truth, I realized that I had gone against the true nature of reality—I had gone against the nature of love. My essence was unlimited love, and in going against this nature I had gone against my own true nature. The pain of this separation, the separation from my-*self*, made me look back at the actions I had done against the nature of love.

I believe that it was my shock of realizing that I had been separated from truth that caused me to have a life-review. In my life-review, I was forced to look at all the pain that I had caused through my negative actions. This review was a flashback, like a movie, playing out all the scenes in my life when I had caused suffering to others. I saw myself being angry and hurting my mother. Then there was a flashback of hurting an ex-girlfriend. I saw myself teasing a younger classmate so ruthlessly she was scarred for the rest of her life. All my negative actions played out right in front of my eyes, only this time I saw and felt the full effect these actions had on the people I had hurt.

My life-review showed me the effects of my anger, selfishness, and cruelty, everything that I had been ignorant about before. In the review, I was forced to experience the pain that I had given to others. The pain of recognizing my culpability was indescribable, and I was totally overpowered by deep regret and remorse.

In his book *Saved by the Light*, Dannion Brinkley writes about the same experience of the negative life-review. He tells us how our perspective changes as we are on the receiving end, and forced to experience the pain of the other person and the effect this pain has. He writes that,

> The depth of emotion I experienced during this life-review was astonishing. Not only could I feel the way both I and the other person had felt when an incident took place, I could also feel the feelings of the next person they reacted to.[4]

Moody reports the same experience and describes how feelings are connected to the life-review: "Even the emotions and feelings associated with the images may be re-experienced as one is viewing them."[5] He also explains how seeing selfish actions leads people to feel repentant: "In this state of heightened awareness, when people saw any selfish acts which they had done they felt extremely repentant."[6]

In this heightened state of awareness that is experienced outside the body, seeing negative actions is extremely painful. As we saw in the last chapter, when we leave the body we enter into a powerful light of unlimited love beyond comprehension. Coming out of Plato's cave, we see everything in its true light. Outside the cave, the sun is shining brightly with peace and love. This is the true nature of existence that before was hidden to us, and we realize that this is our true nature, too. After realizing this, when we then become aware of the fact that we have caused pain and suffering to others, we feel repentant.

The pain of awakening to this is extremely powerful. The sensation is truly out of this dimension, and therefore beyond our comprehension. For me, the only way that I can try to describe the sensation is through the pull of gravity in free fall. When I was younger, I tried bungee jumping, and I remember the feeling of the pull of gravity while I was falling. This pull of gravity, for me, does have some resemblance to the sensation in the out-of-dimension state.

Try to imagine the powerful pull of gravity in free fall. You are falling in empty space. Now imagine that this overpowering force is the pain of knowing that you were ignorant about the true nature of existence. And that you therefore hurt other people, especially people you loved. You had the chance to love, but this chance was lost, and therefore love was lost. Knowing that your true nature is love, you now also realize that you have been lost. All this time, gravity is pulling on you with an overpowering sensation that you have never experienced before.

What is Hell?

There is little doubt that the negative life-review feels like hell. Margot Grey says about the experience that, "The hell-like experience is defined as being one which includes all the elements comprehended in the negative phase (extreme fear or panic, emotional and mental anguish), only more so in that feelings are encountered with a far greater intensity."[7]

Let me be quick to say that in the near-death research, these negative experiences do not happen to everyone. Also there seems to be less insight on why exactly they happen. Some researchers find no accounts or very few of hell-like experiences, like Moody who explains that his subjects have been mostly normal and nice people. Other researchers like Fenwick and Grey found that 15 percent and 12 percent had hellish experiences.[8] P. M. H. Atwater in her large sample of over 3,000 near-death experiences found that 18 percent had "unpleasant experiences," and hereof only a third had experiences that were "truly hellish."[9] What is interesting here is that Atwater found the 15 percent with adults, while only 3 percent with children.

The largest estimate made on life-reviews alone, was made by George Gallup and William Proctor in 1982, who estimated out of 8 million Americans, 2.5 million had experienced "the impression of reviewing or re-examining" their life.[10] This is almost a third of the total number of near-death experiencers and this number is confirmed by Dr. Jeffrey Long who in his research also found about 35 percent had a life-review.[11]

When studying the research I find that there is a distinction between having a life-review, having a life-review with negative contents, and having a deep hell-like experience. Some researchers speculate that negative experiences are harder to come by because people mostly remember positive experiences. I like this explanation because it is very close to my own experience. Fenwick tells us that "about 15 percent did mention moments of terror, although the experience as a whole had been seen as positive."[12]

I think this is a good answer because the pain of my own experience was weighed out by the extremely positive feeling of joy and love from the light. According to Fenwick, "Although actions which have been carried out are often seen as shabby and self-interested, the person does not feel judged; guilt is made more tolerable by the supportive quality of the surrounding light of love."[13]

There is also a theory that the life-review happens to people who suddenly find themselves near death. Kenneth Ring suggested that people in an accident or suffering a heart-attack are more likely to experience a life-review than people who had a near-death experience during a long drawn-out illness. Fenwick also found evidence to support this in that the life-reviews that he found did occur in 'sudden death' situations.[14]

Instead of trying to calculate anyone's chance of having a life-review or 'going to hell,' I would just like to establish that life-reviews and negative experiences do exist. Grey concludes that, "I nevertheless found indicators that pointed to the fact that negative encounters, while infrequent, do however definitely exist."[15] I can affirm this conclusion from my own experience—whether it truly exists or is merely a psychological event, it does happen to some people.

What I mean to say is that even though hell has been misused as a tool to create fear, I do not believe that we can rule out its existence. And even though hell might have been misunderstood and misinterpreted, it does not mean that we should not try to understand it so that we can avoid it. Therefore, I will look into the meaning of hell in the light of my own experience of it in hope that something can be learned from it.

The term *Hell* that we use today can be traced back to the name "Hel" in Norse mythology. Here we find *Hel* as the goddess of the underworld Helheim. The English root is "Helan" and cross-checking this word, we find that it translates into "Celare" in Latin. *Celare* in Latin then translates back into "conceal" or "hidden" in English.[16]

What we now have found is that hell is a hidden and concealed place. This fits with the Greek underworld Hades, which has the same meaning, "Unseen."[17] And this brings us back to Plato's cave again where we can use the allegory to explain what hell is. Living inside the cave as our body, we live in a dark world of illusion made from the shadows of our ignorance.

Outside the cave is the true world that is bathed in the light of the sun. However, this reality is hidden and concealed, because we live in darkness inside the cave. But when we leave the body at the moment of death, we escape the darkness of the cave. Everything that was before unseen is now fully displayed in its true light and glory.

This new world is a powerful revelation, and we are blinded by it. We have been used to the darkness for so long that the true light of existence is too much for our eyes. The true nature of existence outside the cave is beyond our comprehension, and we are totally overwhelmed. The light of the sun shines with infinite love and we are overwhelmed in total humility.

Then, as we regain our eyesight, we look back toward the cave from where we came. We now remember the life that we lived inside the cave. Our lives were filled with delusion from living in the shadow world of the darkness. The darkness caused us to be unaware of reality, and therefore we were selfish, conceited, and proud. This made us cause pain and suffering to others.

Now, from the outside of the cave, we see all of this in its true light, and we realize that we were wrong. We believed in the illusion of the shadows, and in doing so we became lost. Being ignorant, we hurt others, but now we understand that this is not what life is about. The essence of life is far greater and much more profound than we had ever imagined inside the cave. Thus, hell is the pain of looking within and seeing the festering wound from living in the dark nothingness of the cave.

In *The Tibetan Book of the Dead* we find a similar explanation of what happens when we leave the body. Here we find "The Lord of Death," who holds a mirror in which the naked soul is reflected.[18] The mirror is the true light, and this metaphor of a mirror as reflecting the truth is also used in psychology. Carl Jung uses this picture to explain the power of the unconscious to mirror the individual objectively: "Giving him a view of himself that he may never have had before. Only through the unconscious can such a view (which often shocks and upsets the conscious mind) be obtained."[19]

From the Buddhist perspective, the conscious mind is the unenlightened mind, and the unconscious mind is the enlightened mind. Our enlightened nature is the mirror, which objectively reflects our unenlightened nature. To put this in context with the science we looked at earlier, the objective mirror would be the ultimate reality, or our true self as pure consciousness. Our true nature is pure consciousness as the fundamental level of the universe. When the conceptual mind dissolves at the moment of death, the essence of the mind returns to that from which it is produced. The unenlightened constructs of our minds, are dissolved into the true nature of the mind.

In this way, our subjective and relative mind is reflected onto the objective and absolute nature of our mind. What was before hidden in our unconscious mind is now seen as the reflection in our objective mind. In other words, what was unconscious before now becomes conscious. This is the pain of awakening, when our unconscious actions become conscious. And this is possible because in every moment of our lives, our unconscious mind records our actions. When this subconscious memory suddenly becomes conscious, there is an experience of pain from the shocking revelation. This is the pain of looking within and this is the pain of hell.

This revelation can become very painful if our illusion has been very strong because the illusion is a layer of lies that separate us from reality. Sometimes, we believe so strongly in the lie that it becomes the truth for us, and when the real truth is revealed, this delusion becomes painful. For me, the experience of the negative life-review was like being caught lying. I recall as a child the feeling of being discovered not telling the truth. In fact, most of us probably do remember some incident as a child when our parents caught us telling untruthful stories. At that moment when we were exposed, we felt fear and pain. This is the pain of re-entering reality after the layer of the delusion has been removed.

Now imagine a life in which we have built lie upon lie, layer upon layer. In our stubborn ignorance, we have rejected the truth throughout our entire lives. At the moment of death, when we leave the cave, all of these layers come off and we are exposed to the raw truth. This moment will be very painful, and therefore fearful, if we have built up many layers of lies without facing the truth while alive. In that moment when all the layers come off, we free fall into the structure-less, primal state of our existence. This is an experience so far from the delusions of our minds that the exposure of stripping our souls naked causes great fear and pain. And when we find ourselves completely naked looking into the mirror, seeing the images of people we have hurt, we will be struck by overwhelming regret.

Buddhist Soygal Rinpoche explains the experience.

> Whether we like it or not, our true nature is revealed. But it is important to know that there are two aspects of our being that are revealed at the moment of death: our absolute nature, and our relative nature–how we are, and have been, in this life. As the body dies, the senses and subtle elements dissolve, and this is followed by the death of the ordinary aspects of our mind, with all its negative emotions of anger, desire, and ignorance. Finally nothing remains to obscure our true nature, as everything that in life has clouded the enlightened mind has fallen away. And what is revealed is the primordial ground of our absolute nature.[20]

What is Sin?

Having gone through the terror of the negative life-review, there is one element that is very important to observe about the near-death experience: the judgment happens without guilt and punishment. The motive of the judgment is to make people become aware, not to punish or place blame. In Rumi's poem, it is the pain of looking within that saves us — the intention of the pain is to save us by making us aware.

Dannion Brinkley tells us that "I had felt the pain and anguish of reflection, but from that I had gained the knowledge that I could use to correct my life."[21] This was also my experience, and it is also a general conclusion of the near-death research: "the sense of judgment and guilt does not exist."[22] Becoming aware of our negative actions happens within a source of unlimited love. Moody found that there is no accusation or threat because people "feel total love and acceptance coming from the light." And, therefore, the review is more a kind of Socratic questioning to make the person "proceed along the path to the truth by himself."[23]

The positive feelings of peace and joy are the most common emotions in the near-death experience, reported by 88 percent of people who have had near-death experiences. And as I mentioned before, Fenwick also finds that even among those who suffered a negative life-review, 15 percent, the near-death experience as a whole had been positive.[24] This is an important finding that fits perfectly with my own experience. The fundamental nature of reality, our absolute nature of mind, has this quality of peace, joy, and love.

Brinkley explains that this can be compared to the non-judgmental compassion that a grandfather has for a grandchild. This is the same as in Buddhism where the mother meets the child—we are the children and the light is our mother. When we return to our mother, we are greeted with love and compassion. Therefore, in the near-death experience, "most of the individuals interviewed did not experience any reward-punishment crisis."[25]

To make this point clearer, I will look into what it means to sin. Father Laurence Freedman opens the door to a deep understanding of what sin is by saying, "The Greek for sin means to miss the target. Sin is what turns consciousness away form truth. Being the consequence of illusion and selfishness, sin includes its own punishment. God does not do the punishing."[26]

This statement fits very well with another near-death experiencer who explains that, "Nobody judges you; you judge yourself...Nobody says 'you've been bad'...You know better than anyone, because it's your thoughts and your motives...And one gets precisely and exactly what one deserves. It's utterly fair."[27]

The Greek term for sin means that as an archer misses his target with his arrow, so our consciousness misses the target of the truth. The target of our consciousness is to be conscious and aware. If we miss this target, we "go wrong" or "fail to do, neglect."[28] Another old Greek meaning of the word "sin" is that "I should lose my sight by Ulysses' hand."[29] Here, sin means to be blind of the truth, and it is due to our blindness that we sin. This blindness leads a person to "fail of one's purpose,"[30] which again matches my experience of the negative life-review perfectly.

This makes us see a sinner as someone who is blind because the person's consciousness is turned away from truth, and, thus, the purpose of this person's life has failed. Now, if we look at the biblical term, "The Fall of Man," this in Greek is translated as "failure" or "error of judgment."[31] Man has fallen by failing the purpose of life due to error in judgment. From this perspective leaving the Garden of Eden means that we have left our essence—the knowledge of who we are. Disconnected from our souls, we live in ignorance of our true nature, and this causes us to suffer.

We also find this conclusion in *The Gnostic Gospels* where Elaine Pagels explains that,

> Remaining unaware of their own selves, they have no root. *The Gospel of Truth* describes such existence as a nightmare. Those who live in it experience terror and confusion and instability and doubt and division, being caught in many illusions. Whoever remains ignorant, a creature of oblivion, cannot experience fulfillment.[32]

This is how, disconnected from our root (our soul), man is "being driven by impulses he does not understand."[33] Man has fallen by disconnecting from the root and inner essence. In this confusion, man is letting his primal nature run him, through competing and fighting for survival. Lost in this nightmare of terror and war, he has forgotten who he truly is and where he comes from.

This was also my story. I had become lost in a material world, without knowing my essence. In this emptiness, I was hurting others with my ignorance. Waking up from this nothingness was an extremely painful experience, and following my negative life-review, I felt I had gone against love and my true nature. I had missed the whole point of life, and in doing so, my life had gone wrong.

The Buddhists call the mirror—"mirror of evolution." Something wants to evolve through us. Something wants to grow. Moody explains that many near-death experiencers have returned with the vision of learning that the "development of the soul, especially in the spiritual faculties of love and knowledge, does not stop on earth. Rather, it continues on the other side."[34] The ultimate reality, our essence, is pulling us toward it. The light shines with unlimited love, calling our name. The light wants us to learn and grow into the nature of love. This is what all the religions tell us, and this is also the message from the near-death experience. If we choose to live with love and compassion, we flow with the true nature of existence. If we choose to go against the flow, we will have to face the consequences some day.

In a different connection, Wayne W. Dyer uses these words of Mother Theresa, "You see, in the final analysis, it is all between you and God."[35] For me, this line captures what it is all about. We cannot escape the transition of death, so in this final analysis of our lives, the only thing that matters is whether we have lived our lives according to the true nature of existence. Therefore, the purpose of life is stated clearly as living in harmony with our essence.

It is only when we reject this truth that we go against the flow of the universe. The Quran states that, "Those who reject truth will be in Hell-fire."[36] Rejecting truth is a choice, and therefore God does not do the punishing. Even though God gave us free will, he is not responsible for our choices. By rejecting truth, we turn our consciousness away from reality, and through this error in judgment we fail the purpose of life. Thus, the separation from our true nature, our essence, is painful. It is our choice of separation that creates the pain, when we awaken to the truth.

Now we can see sin as false consciousness—'evil' is ignorance. And the punishment for sin is the pain of becoming conscious of our delusion. This is the awakening of our consciousness, from the false view to the right view. In chapter six, I explained how this awakening is an essential part of meditation. By looking within, we experience the true nature of our mind, and on this foundation we awaken from the false concepts. In the same way, dying is an awakening after life where we awaken to the true nature of reality. When we die, we become reunited with our true nature, the mother of all things, and in this reunion the unenlightened mind is purified.[37]

This is also what we found earlier in science. The fundamental reality is consciousness. When we die, the constructs of our mind fall away, and the true nature of our mind appears. The energy of consciousness is constant; therefore, when the relative concepts of our minds fall away, our essence of pure consciousness is all that remains. "The mind energy is literally recycled in the environment."[38]

This is similar to the phase transition of water from ice to steam when a substance is transformed from one state to another. The transition of the mind energy happens by crossing the boundary of this dimension and entering another. Only the pure mind energy can return to its source, and therefore we experience the pain of the conceptual (polluted) mind as it dissolves and is left behind.

However, as Rumi points out, the delusion is a divine curse. From our source, we enter this world, and we are born into the Original Sin. This delusion was here before we came into the world. This is why Danish philosopher Kierkegaard pointed out that Adam was innocent. Just because Adam was able to speak, it does not follow that he was also able to understand the full meaning of the words spoken by God. Due to Adam's fear of the unknown, he was like a child who had to learn from his own experience. That the fruit was forbidden made the fear in him push his free will to overcome the unknown, and thereby escape his fear.[39]

Therefore, ignorance is innocence and if the Church had chosen the Gnostic interpretation of the words of Jesus, there would have been no 'evil' in our world today. The Gnostics told us that "ignorance, not sin, is what involves a person in suffering." It is because man lacks self-knowledge, the knowledge of his true nature, that he is being driven by impulses that he is unable to understand. It is not because he fully understands the words of God—is enlightened as God—and still intentionally chooses to do 'evil.'

Truth and Separation

Now that we have gone through a different understanding of what hell might be, and what it feels like, I will look into where this judgment comes from. Here I will just rephrase the quote of Father Freedman, "Being the consequence of illusion and selfishness, sin includes its own punishment. God does not do the punishing."[40]

So where then does this punishment come from? The Hebrew word for hell is "Sheol," and it takes us in this direction. The root of this word is "Shaal," which means "to ask" or "to inquire."[41] In most religions, we find the Lord, God, or some servant inquires. In many accounts of near-death experiences, we also find that a being of light or an angel leads the person through the life-review.

For me, my experience was different. I was alone with myself, and it was me passing judgment on myself. Another near-death experience describes the inquirer in a way that is very similar to my experience, "It was me judging me, not some heavenly Saint Peter."[42] This is also the view of Moody, who concludes that the judgment comes from within.[43] We also find this perspective on the nature of reality in Buddhism, where Soygal Rinpoche says, "Ultimately all judgments take place within our own mind. We are the judge and the judged."[44]

This means that from an absolute perspective, the negative life-review is created by our own mind. The fundamental reality of the universe is consciousness beyond the construct of the negative review. Enlightenment, or absolute consciousness, is the ultimate nature of existence, and is free of any construct of the conditioned mind. We also find that near-death researchers agree with this view. Grey explains that, "In all the 'core experiences', respondents quite categorically state that there was no sense of judgment, that any judgment came from themselves."[45] And Fenwick concludes that, "It does look quite possible that in the NDE, as in life, we tend to create our own Heaven or Hell."[46]

Not only do we create our experience of hell, but there is also evidence to suggest that our environment impacts the negative experience. A German study on near-death experiences found a big difference in the negative experience in the near-death experience between West and East Germany. In this study 29 percent of West German near-death experiencers had a negative experience, while 60 percent of the East German near-death experiencers had a negative experience.[47]

This suggests that both mental and cultural conditioning in a person's environment does affect the near-death experience. So, if we create our own hell and our environment can have an influence on its negative content, should we then not disregard hell as purely illusion? It could be that hell is merely a religious creation that has no inherent reality of its own.

Well, some people would probably think so, but I truly believe that it is not that simple. It is true that among some other cultures, like Aboriginal and First Nations peoples the research, so far, does not find life-reviews in the near-death experience. This could suggest that the life-review is a conditioning that comes from our Western culture, which would be a very interesting subject for future research.

However, even though these non-Western cultures seem to have a lack of life-reviews, they still have negative experiences. One aboriginal study of near-death experiences by Dr. Nsama Mumbwe of the University of Zambia found no life-reviews. But as Melvin Morse explains, "many of these African people interpreted the event as somewhat evil. Half of the participants in this simple study thought that the NDE signified that they were 'bewitched' or about to be."[48]

So, however we choose to interpret the experience, it looks as if we still do find negative experiences in all cultures. Therefore, I would suggest that the experience is a mental projection and an illusion to the enlightened mind. But unless a person is fully enlightened or only doing good actions, I do not believe that the possibility of having a negative life-review or a negative experience can be completely disregarded.

Grey tells us that, "My view is that this refers to 'unfinished business' that has become trapped in the psyche or soul and which continues to cause problems until recognized and overcome."[49] Now, when the purpose of the life-review seems to be that the person learns, and this teaching of the soul seems to continue after life, my question would be: When do we have no more unfinished business? The answer to me would be when we are fully enlightened.

About the learning part, Moody explains that the point of the questioning seems to be "to draw them out," and that the Socratic questioning is not to acquire information, "but to help the person who is being asked to proceed along the path to the truth about himself."[50] Moody uses the words "provoke reflection,"[51] and for me, it is clear that provoking reflection must contain unknown or forgotten events.

One account testifies that, "I experienced the review of my life which extended from early childhood and included many occurrences that I had completely forgotten."[52] This happened to me as well, especially the incident where I was teasing a girl in 5th grade. I had totally forgotten this event, and becoming aware of it was a shock to me.

Since this is a psychological event, I will look to Carl Jung to try and understand it. He describes the transference of death as the union of the conscious and unconscious. When the soul is "withdrawn from projections and reunites with the body, a bridge is formed for access between the conscious and unconscious, leading to the Self."[53]

This withdrawal from projection, leading to the unconscious, can be dangerous: "Another danger is that, when integrated, the contents of the unconscious may so enlarge the ego that one runs the risk of an inflation."[54] Jung further explains about the unconscious: "Because the latter cannot be seen directly, it is always projected; for, unlike the shadow, it does not belong to the ego but is collective. For this reason it is felt to be something alien to us."[55]

In my view, it is clear that the strong and enlightened mind can stir out of the negative review and into liberation. But since unconscious actions and long forgotten events also come up in this intense out-of-dimension state, the mind would need to be strong or free of big surprises. If we have lived a life being responsible for huge suffering or the killing of others, it seems to me that this ignorance will bounce off the true nature of reality—something "alien"—which so profoundly expresses unending love. These harmful actions must be healed before this meeting—otherwise I see no other outcome than a big shock, which can lock the mind in a negative state.

Therefore, I believe that the negative life-review should be not feared but respected, so that one does not have to run the risk of ego inflation. Avoiding inflation is not always as simple as we might think because—as Jung puts it—identification, which causes inflation, is "always tempting the ego." This is due to our habitual tendencies of identifying with the projections, and therefore, "Non-identification demands considerable moral effort."[56]

On this issue Soygal Rinpoche, who also has studied the near-death experience, explains that, "The life-review happens again and again in the near-death experience, and demonstrates so clearly the inescapability of karma and the far-reaching and powerful effects of all our actions, words, and thoughts."

Yet it would seem that many people are frolicking down the same path of ignorance that I trod prior to my experience. Let me just bring back the results from The Barna Group poll which found that "Truth is Relative, says Americans."[57] Here, 64 percent of adult Americans said that, "truth is always relative to the person and their situation." With teenagers this view was even more extreme, 83 percent said that, "moral truth depends on the circumstances." Only 22 percent of adults and 6 percent of teenagers said that moral truth is absolute.[58]

What is interesting about the survey is that it was done after the terrorist attacks on September 11, and that condemning the 'evil' of these attacks seemed to lack no conviction in the foundational belief in an absolute of right and wrong. And at the same time, studies continuously show that about 90 percent of Americans believe in God or some higher power.[59] Even so, the poll found that more than 60 percent of Americans "endorse relativism," and the survey suggests that without a firm basis for moral decision-making, people are left with "philosophies such as 'if it feels good, do it,' 'everyone else is doing it' or the 'whatever' among young people."[60]

For me, this is very alarming. When I look at the news on TV, I am deeply sad by all the death and destruction. I cry when I think of the all the suffering we cause in life and of the consequences after. The Bible tells us that it is better to lose one part of our body than for our whole body to go to hell.[61] While cutting off the hand that causes us to sin is too extreme in my view, I do feel the seriousness these words are trying to express. Personally, I try hard to do the right thing, and not cause suffering to others, because I respect life and I do not wish to go through another negative life-review.

Then when I look at the world we live in and I think about the true nature of the light, I am deeply horrified. From my experience of the light, I truly believe that no human being is worth less than another, and no one deserves to suffer much less being killed. It seems very clear to me that killing is against the true nature of life, exactly as the Bible tells us: Thou shall not kill.

The nature of life is to live. For this reason, it is in our nature to seek to be happy. We all desire to be happy, because we all desire to live. This is universal for all life, and is therefore a universal principle. If we hurt others who also seek to be happy, we are going against this universal principle. In the right to happiness, we are all equal. By hurting others, we therefore not only go against their nature but also our own true nature. By killing another we kill ourselves.

The Buddhist text *The Dhammapada* describes this principle in a simple way: "He who, seeking his own happiness, punishes or kills beings who also long for happiness, will not find happiness after death."[62] This we also find in the near-death experience, where Grey explains that, "This sentiment has also been expressed by a number of people who had 'core experiences' who said...that all life is sacred, that to take the life of oneself or another is attended with very severe penalties."[63]

My actions were very selfish, but I have never killed anyone. However, Brinkley, who was a soldier in war, has; and he lets us know how this feels in the life-review:

> I was hit by a rush of emotions and information. I felt the stark horror that all of those people felt...I experienced the pain their families felt when they discovered that they had lost loved ones in such a tragic way. In many cases I even felt the loss their absence would make to future generations...I thought what I was doing was right. (I was killing in the name of patriotism) ...Now, in the life review, I was forced to see the death and destruction that had taken place in the world as a result of my actions. "We are all a link in the great chain of humanity," said the Being. "What you do has an effect on the other links in that chain.[64]

With this information, it seems clear to me that for example the way we do modern warfare, where more civilians die than soldiers, there must be consequences to pay. We cannot stay blind forever of the fact that this is unjust. I do not believe that anyone is totally free of responsibility: The soldier, the general, the government, the arms dealer, and maybe even the voter—we are all links in that great chain of humanity and as Brinkley explains,

> My task was simply to transfer these weapons...When this transfer was completed, I got back on the airplane and left. But leaving wasn't so easy in my life review. I stayed with the weapons and watched as they were distributed at a military staging area. Then I went with the guns as they were used in the job of killing, some of them murdering

innocent people...All in all it was horrible to witness the results of my role in this war...I knew these deaths were caused by the guns I had delivered.[65]

This conclusion I am making here, might be going too far for some people. But the life-review is as unimaginably intense as the true light of reality is incredibly meaningful. We all know war is wrong, and therefore, we must stop doing war. Life is profoundly meaningful. When we leave it we will experience just how profound it is and how much is recorded:

> There was no denying the facts because they were all there, including my innermost thoughts, emotions and motives. I knew that my life was over and whatever came next would be a direct consequence of not only what I had done in my life, but what I had thought and what had been my true feeling at the time.[66]

Now, I will go back to the title of this sub-chapter: Truth and Separation. After having lead this part of the chapter to another view on who does the 'punishment' and 'judgment,' I believe that it is also important to clarify these concepts in the light. As I began with the poem of Rumi it is the pain of looking within that fits with the near-death experience.

For me, this pain was clearly caused by recognizing that I was separate from the truth. Here again Greek thinking can help us understand this. As we saw, hell is a hidden and concealed place and if we look at the word "truthful" in Greek it also means "unconcealed." Opposite untruthful would then mean concealed and that brings the meaning of hell in direct relationship with truth as its opposite. In this way, hell can be seen as the separation from truth and this fits perfectly with my personal experience of it.

Thereby, hell is the pain of separation from truth or from God. This is the important distinction that leads away from punishment and sin, to the understanding that the pain comes out of ignorance. I also used the example of Adam being innocent because he was unenlightened and ignorant of the meaning of the words of God.

However, I also believe that it is important to say that innocence does not mean that we are not responsible. We are only ignorant of what we do not know but responsible for what we do know. This means that our innocence is over once we become aware of the truth. If we know the truth but do not act upon it, then, this is corruption, and it is this corruption that creates the separation. If we were always truthful and true to ourselves there would be no sin. This is what Jesus means when he says that "there is no sin, but it is you who make sin."[67]

Plato said the same when he explained that "the responsibility is with the chooser."[68] The seed of creation springs from our mind; thus, we are responsible for what we think. This brings us back to Mother Teresa again; who after saying that in the final analysis it is all between you and God, also said: "It was never between you and them anyway."[69] In our world today, it is easy to be caught up in the world 'out there,' but even so, we are still responsible in here. We sin, or manifest false consciousness, through corruption. When we know something to be true and we do not act accordingly, then we are no longer ignorant.

Fenwick comes to this conclusion as well: "We need a wider view to encompass...that we are part of a greater whole, and that our actions carry personal responsibility and have consequences for us or for the universe at some future time."[70] He shares this view with His holiness, the Dalai Lama, who explains that our actions have a universal dimension—a universal responsibility. The human family has a fundamental unity, and we cannot view our interests as separate from those of others. [71]

A good example is global warming. Greedy businesses have done everything possible to deny that we are all connected through nature. Another example is the poverty and suffering in our world. While some have too much, others have nothing, and *everyday* thousands die because of their lack. But in the true nature of the light no form of life is worth less than another, and no human race is more valuable than another.

In his book *The End of Poverty*, Jeffrey Sachs explains that our rich part of the world is saying to the poor that "you count for nothing. We should not be surprised, then, if in later years the rich reap the whirlwind of that heartless response."[72] I believe that as long as the rich of our world consume the energy of the poor of the world, there will be no end to hell. "For I was hungry and you gave me nothing to eat, I was thirsty and you gave me nothing to drink."[73]

When we look at the world today it is clear that greed, plunder, and killing are still legitimate means of doing business. Man's short-term goal is for his own survival, here and now. As our last century saw us evolve from the Enlightenment to Auschwitz, it is evident that humanity faces a problem. Philosopher Jacques Derrida explains that our newfound freedom has an active and militant aspect that is to be found in all levels of society.[74]

Maybe this militant aspect is part of human nature, but during the last century when we were supposed to become more enlightened, we have developed new ways to kill one another in greater numbers. Since our Western society became secular by the dismissal of God and Darwin's theory of natural selection lead us to the survival of the fittest, it seems as if we have legitimized the destruction of humanity as "natural selection." Enlightenment has brought us freedom, but this freedom has been mistaken as unconditional freedom to kill and destroy.

In doing so, man is disregarding the long-term consequences for all of us. Freedom is not unconditional because we are responsible for our actions. This is the clear message from the near-death experience, and I believe if we all look deep within, we will find this to be true.

What will it take to wake man up and see the big picture?

Lost in No-Man's Land

Now, I said before that the negative review unfolds with love, in a dimension with a source behind it of unlimited love. And even the people who had negative experiences said that the NDE as a whole had been positive. But even so, it still seems possible to become lost in the negative review.

The Greek underworld, Hades, is described as an "intermediate place for all souls until final judgment."[75] I think this statement "until final judgment" is important in the old discussion on whether hell is eternal damnation. Margot Grey tells us that, "So far the experiences we have described, while being nightmarish, are still not exactly in line with the concept of 'burning forever in the fires of hell'."[76]

For me, the Biblical term *purgatory*, where one is cleansed before admission to heaven, seems to be much more fitting than eternal damnation. I do prefer the parallel with the life-review that makes the experience similar to that of a lifetime. However, at the same time I must admit that I do not have any way of knowing whether it is possible to be lost forever in no-man's land, since it is beyond my personal experience.

In this intermediate place, we find a place of punishment that resembles the biblical hell. This place is called "Tartarus," and is translated as "demonic powers who seek to oppose passage of souls to heaven."[77] I would like to interpret these "demonic powers" that oppose our passage to heaven as the negative mind states in the negative review. This is the power of the illusion as the layers of lies that we talked about before. If the lie is too strong, we become trapped inside the "demonic powers" of the illusion.

Other near-death experiences have described these lost souls as "trapped" and "bewildered." They are trapped because they are "unable to surrender their attachment to the physical world." "They seem to be caught in between somewhere. It's neither spiritual nor physical. It's a level somewhere between the two."[78]

This sounds a lot like a situation we have all experienced in our own minds. All of us have at some point in our lives had bad times, and experienced deep pain and confusion. The confusion creates a split between the real and the unreal; the greater the split, the greater the illusion in our minds. In our pain, we cling on to the delusion, and through our fear we manifest the unreal.

This is the unstable mind that has lost its foundation in reality. Without the right view on reality within our minds, we become lost in our minds' false concepts. We project our pain onto the world outside, and the reflection we receive back is as dark as what we send out. This is how we manifest our own hell through the power of our minds: "It looks like they have lost the knowledge of who they are, what they are" — "They seem to be trying to decide."[79]

Leaving our bodies when we die, the negative mind states can become even more negative through increased fear. After my experience, I entered a time of confusion. Before, I knew only one reality, but now I had experienced another far more powerful. For this reason, I was split between the two realities: the reality of my conceptual mind and the reality I had experienced beyond. With the help of my psychotherapist, I quickly regained my grounding in this world again. But having experienced the split between the two realities, I can imagine how we can become lost in this out-of-body state. The reality of this state is simply far too powerful for our minds, and, therefore, out of fear we go deeper inside the illusion to hide.

In Plato's cave allegory, this would be coming out of the cave and seeing the sunlight for the first time. Looking straight at the light for the first time would make the unprepared person take refuge in the objects already known. What we conceive by habit would therefore seem more real, and therefore someone would go back into the cave and hide in the darkness.

Soygal Rinpoche explains how we get lost in this way: "We will remain imprisoned in the very aspect of ourselves that has to die. This ignorance will rob us of the basis of the journey to enlightenment, and trap us endlessly in the realm of illusion."[80]

In *What Survives?* Michael Grosso says that not all of us are spiritually ready to meet this ultimate reality. In fact, the less prepared we are, the more we would react with fear, and recoil from such a meeting.[81] This could explain why some people so firmly disregard the possibility of there being life after death. Maybe their last encounter was so fearful that this fear now makes them reject the possibility in this life.

In Plato's cave, we also find that the prisoners fight against their liberation. First, they react with disbelief to hearing about the reality outside the cave. Then, when the one who was outside the cave tries to liberate the others, they put him to death. But the truth outside the cave cannot be ignored forever. We are being pulled toward evolution, and what is pulling us and our whole universe will not stop.

Whether someone is lost in this world or in the in-between dimension, this power pushes us to heal the pain. In the old days, the Shamans sent the lost spirits home, in order to restore balance to nature. Today, we are finally realizing that our planet is a living organism, and that we cannot live in an irresponsible manner. We are also learning that the Earth is round, which means that we cannot run away or escape the problems we face. We are all entangled and share a fundamental oneness through our ultimate nature. Everything is connected beyond our comprehension and we are all in this together.

Having gone deep into the darkest corner of hell, I wish to point back to the great hope of our world. In the evolution of consciousness there is great hope to be found. As our world evolves—so does the human race. It also seems that there could be a corresponding evolution going on in hell. In the book *Sleeping, Dreaming, and Dying,* Joan Halifax tells us that medieval accounts of near-death experiences have more guilt and judgment than today's experiences. She says that, "unlike in the medieval accounts, the sense of judgment or guilt does not exist" for people who have near-death experiences today.[82]

What does this mean? Well, it could follow the evolution in our understanding of religion or merely show a difference in the language that we use to describe the experience. However, it could also seem possible that as we evolve, so too, does the negative life-review. As we evolve, so too, does our consciousness about what negative actions are. It would make sense that with evidence from the near-death experience that the learning of the soul continues, then the contents of the life-review as the ultimate teaching tool would also have to evolve.

When I think of the way we treat our planet, pollution, the rate of extinction, and how we treat animals, in this relation I feel the future potential for negative consequences. Dannion Brinkley writes, "Later, as I thought about these experiences, I realized that people who beat animals or are cruel to them are going to know how those animals felt when they have a life-review."[83]

I believe that the big crisis that humanity is experiencing, such as the effects of global warming and the consequences of our decision to go to war, are leaving behind open wounds to teach us about our ignorance. Everything is connected—all is one—and if we do not learn in life while here on earth, we will have to learn the hard way when we die.

Chapter Nine

The Golden Rule

Native American:

"Respect for all life is the foundation."[1]

Judaism:

"Love thy neighbor as thyself."[2]

Christianity:

"Do to others what you would have them do to you."[3]

Islam:

"Wish for others what you wish for yourself."[4]

Confucianism:

"Do not do to others what you would not have them do to you."[5]

Hinduism:

"Do not do to others what would cause pain if done to you."[6]

Buddhism:

"A state that is not pleasing or delightful to me, how could I inflict that upon another?"[7]

The Golden Rule is found in most religions as a universal statement about the nature of life. To explain the profound meaning of love from the light is impossible, but I believe that the Golden Rule is a good interpretation of the light. Just as the near-death experiencer cannot put into words the true nature of the light, no religion can either. But still both the near-death experience and religion can point to the light. I am thereby convinced that they are both authentic responses to the light and the ultimate nature of reality. To me, the Golden Rule is the most authentic response to the light, and it sums up the law on how we should align ourselves with the ultimate reality: To love each other as the light loves us.

The Golden Rule is also called the Ethic of Reciprocity, meaning mutual exchange. Reciprocity is the mutual exchange or dependence, and to reciprocate means to give and take mutually.[8] We can also say that what you send out comes back to you, and thereby the Golden Rule is the universal law of balance. This makes sense since the entire universe, from the smallest organism to the largest galaxy, seeks harmony and balance through the fine-tuning of the universe.

Near-death researcher, Kenneth Ring, let us know that the lessons learned from the life-review are evidence of the interconnectedness of everything in the universe. Ring explains that its reason for being can "be understood as a basic principle of life from which standpoint the Golden Rule is a logical derivative."[9]

The evidence of quantum entanglement in science tells us that all things are interconnected. This interconnectedness means that the universe receives the consequences of our actions, and therefore, our actions have implications and effects. The Golden Rule as a universal law of balance teaches us this basic principle of life through the life-review, and the near-death experience testifies that this could very well be the basic law of how the universe works.

We already know the Golden Rule from religion, and now in our time, thousands people come back from their meetings with the light and confirm our beliefs.

One near-death experiencer came back with this heartfelt message from the light:

> I wish everyone could have one—it would change the world! Everyone would understand each other, and there wouldn't be conflict, and there wouldn't be chaos, and there wouldn't be greed and war...The life review is the ultimate teaching tool.[10]

Bruce Greyson explains that to the near-death experiencer "the Golden Rule is no longer just a commandment one is taught to obey, but rather an indisputable law of nature, as inevitable as gravity."[11] He concludes from his thirty years of research that

> The bulk of the evidence points towards that after you leave the body, the soul becomes much less individualized and starts to emerge with something larger than itself—that we are all potentially a part of...we are all part of the same thing. If we thought that we were eternal and more important than that, that we are all interconnected, that as Jesus said; what you are doing to me, you are doing to yourself...If we really believed that that is the way the universe worked, we wouldn't be perpetrating such horrors on each other.[12]

Science, which dictates the point of view of the Western world today, has its mainstream belief in the classical view of Darwinism. This belief has turned into what we call Social Darwinism, where science is eroding our moral foundation through its conservative belief in survival of the fittest. While nature alone does evolve around survival, this small piece of our universe makes social Darwinist believe that this raw nature is all that there is in our infinite universe.

Speaking of the Golden Rule, Charles Darwin said in *The Descent of Man* that

> Social instincts—the prime principle of man's moral constitution— with the aid of active intellectual powers and the effects of habit, naturally lead to the golden rule, "As ye would that men should do to you, do ye to them likewise;" and this lies at the foundation of morality.[13]

This was written in 1871 at a time when America had just been built by slaves after it was taken from the Native Americans. To me, Darwin's thinking clearly reflects a colonial worldview that is set in a time of greed and corruption. I do not see how this kind of thinking (which was based on the study of primitive animals) could have discovered the full mystery of the universe.

Darwin's argument that the Golden Rule is merely a social instinct is the classic foundation of skepticism, and to this kind of skepticism even love is merely a "social construct." This way of thinking would provide a convenient alibi in colonial times where we would have to look the other way to avoid being horrified by our actions. But if the message from the light truly tells us something about the underlying nature of reality, then this kind of thinking has enormous implications for us all.

In the *Emperor's New Mind,* Roger Penrose says:

> It is hard for me to believe, as some have tried to maintain, that such SUPERB theories [Platonic values] could have arisen merely by some random natural selection of ideas leaving only the good ones as survivors. The good ones are simply much *too* good to be the survivors of ideas that have arisen in that random way. There must, indeed, be some deep underlying reason.[14]

Penrose sees morality as a fundamental element that is absolute and independent of individuals or cultures. He also explains that morality intertwined with consciousness seems to be fundamental, and that we therefore ultimately cannot separate the Platonic world from the mental world.[15]

This to me is a much more reasonable description of the structure of the universe than the conclusions of Darwin. Even without the evidence from the near-death experience, most of us feel that love and respect are part of a deeper nature. We feel it and see it in action without being able to fully understand it. That the love we feel deep within our hearts should be merely a superficial illusion seems to be far from our experience. There must indeed be some underlying reason for its existence.

In her book *The Great Transformation,* Karen Armstrong talks about this deep underlying reason. She tells us that "The Golden Rule is the bedrock of spirituality," and that love and compassion is the way we come into contact with the ultimate reality. She also explains that the truth of the Golden Rule is revealed if we put it into practice in our daily lives.[16]

Luckily, this underlying nature of love does seem to have revealed itself to many Americans. As I said earlier, half of the U.S. population says that they have felt "God's presence or a spiritual force" very close to them many times.[17] And with 90 percent of Americans believing in God or some higher power, there is a very strong conviction that a spiritual force is present in our universe.

Armstrong also reminds us that the introduction of compassion was the great transformation in our human evolution. The fact that the Golden Rule emerged independently but simultaneously all over the world tells us that humanity discovered something important about the way human beings worked. Thereby Armstrong concludes that, "The Golden Rule may tell us something important about the structure of our nature."[18]

I am convinced that she is right because this is what we can learn from the near-death experience. Peter Fenwick tells us that some people who have a near-death experience feel that they have "seen through the very texture of the universe into its ultimate structure."[19] He also explains that "the essence" of each of these experiences is the emotional state of love, joy, and peace, which as a feeling state is at the heart of the experience. The peace and oneness of the homecoming comes from a state of being that has always been know and is experienced as an "underlying consciousness."[20]

After having studied over 3,000 cases of near-death experiences, Atwater concludes that, "Powerful in their ability to transform lives, the episodes are somehow 'instructive' about the true reality that exists."[21] And adds that, "While investigating the phenomenon, I have always been impressed that, once you peel away the research data and everyone's opinion about the stories, what remains is really all about ...*love*."[22]

For me, the essence of the near-death experience is without a doubt love—that is really what life is all about. This is the true nature of reality experienced through the light. And while many of us live inside the dark cave where the convenient notions of the shadows have us forget our true nature, I believe as Kenneth Ring does that the awakening message from the light represents an evolutionary thrust toward a higher consciousness for humanity at large.[23]

Margot Grey tells us that the ever-increasing frequency of the near-death experience could be directly related to the evolutionary process, and she also says that, "It could be that higher consciousness is attempting to alert us on a collective level to the urgent need for a universal brotherhood, based on love and goodwill, manifesting compassion."[24]

It seems very possible that the near-death experience today provides us with direct testimony of the underlying nature of reality that the religions have been talking about for thousands of years. Soygal Rinpoche lets us know just how similar the near-death experience is to the message of religion:

> The central message that the near-death experiencers bring back from their encounter with death, or the presence of being of 'light,' is exactly the same as that of Buddha and of the Bardo teachings:

that the essential and most important qualities in life are love and knowledge, compassion and wisdom.[25]

The Light is Love

The Bible tells us that "God is Love,"[26] and that love is the way to experience God: "No one has ever seen God; but if we love one another, God lives in us and his love is made complete in us."[27] When we look deeper into the Golden Rule, this is also what we find at its core.

In a dark time for the Church in the 15th century, not long after the Crusades, Cardinal Nicolas of Cusa said something important that we still need to learn. He summed up how the core of the Golden Rule can be reduced to love:

> The divine commandments are very brief and are well known and common in every nation, for the light that reveals them to us is created along with the rational soul. For within us God says to love Him, from whom we receive being, and to do nothing to another, except that which we wish done to us. Love is therefore, the fulfillment of the law of God and all laws are reduced to this.[28]

The light, as our true nature, is the source from which we receive our being. This is also the profound message from the near-death experience. Kenneth Ring tells us that the greatest lesson from the experience is that the NDE teaches us that "everything *is* love, and is made of love, and comes from love."[29]

This point is illustrated by a near-death experiencer who reveals that, "The Light told me everything was love, and I mean everything! I had always felt love was just a human emotion people felt from time to time, never in my wildest dreams thinking that it was literally *everything!*"[30]

This is truly what it is—it is *all* Love. But when I say love, I do not mean merely the kind of love that we can measure and quantify. I mean an unconditional LOVE beyond our comprehension, as infinite as the size of the universe. It is a love beyond good or bad, beyond right or wrong, it is absolute unconditional love or as Caroline Myss explains:

> Indeed, they "experienced" God, past the intellectual babble about what God is and isn't and what God "thinks" and "doesn't think." They literally went right to the source, only to discover, as they all report, that God apparently doesn't "think" at all. Reports from

near-deathers seem to indicate that upon death we are met with an indescribable sensation of unconditional love.[31]

This was the essence of my experience and the sole motivation for me to write this book. Having had the experience that this *is* the true nature of reality, I look at the world and see so much separation from this nature. As the life-review works to teach us the ultimate truth, I speak this truth out of compassion for those who are separate from it.

The near-death experience testifies that the purpose of life is getting to know God—learning to love. Near-death experiencers and researchers alike agree that the near-death experience is really about life,[32] and Bruce Greyson explains that the purpose of the near-death experience is "to change you, and to inspire you to change your world."[33]

Raymond Moody comes to the same conclusion, revealing that the life-review stresses the importance of, "Learning to love other people and acquire knowledge."[34] This conclusion is echoed by Elisabeth Kübler-Ross, who from her long experience working in hospices tells us that "The sole purpose of life is to grow. The ultimate lesson is learning how to love and be loved *unconditionally*."[35]

And we also find Margot Grey who says that, "It would seem that, however the NDE is brought about, the prime purpose of returning to physical life is to gain an opportunity to try to live life in accordance with the knowledge obtained while on the threshold of death."[36]

But how is someone to believe all these stories from the other side when this person has not been there? Greyson comes up with the answer to this skeptical question. He says: "How can we discern whether NDErs are truly blessed by divine light or deceived by the Prince of Darkness? No less an authority than Jesus gave us the methodology when he said, 'By their fruits ye shall know them' (Matthew 7:20)."[37]

The evidence of this is clearly shown through the significant life-changes that follow the near-death experience. The fruit of the near-death experience grows from the essence of the experience which is love, and that we can see directly in the change in people's lives.

Most researchers find a very significant increase in religious feelings among people after the experience. Peter Fenwick found that 90 percent of adult accounts he studied were more religious,[38] and Kenneth Ring, found that 85 percent of his accounts said that religious feelings had either "strongly increased" or "increased."[39] Ring also found that 95 percent said that their compassion for others had either strongly increased or increased.[40] Tolerance for others was either strongly increased or increased by 84 percent,[41] and 92 percent said that their feelings of love for others had strongly increased or increased.[42]

And finally, 88 percent said that their feelings of wanting to help others had also strongly increased or increased,[43] and the same number found a strong increase or increase in the feeling of the sacredness of life.[44]

What do these increased positive values tell us? Researcher, Melvin Morse, has made the point that there is a connection between the light and these life-changes: "The deeper the experience of the light, the greater the transformation."[45] Also Greyson explains that in evaluating the near-death experience according to his NDE scale, he finds that the overall score on the scale "is highly correlated with many aftereffects."[46]

This is the same for me. I have been totally reborn (re-ne) after my experience. I am a completely different person after my experience with the light. I will have to admit I am in no way superhuman; I still have problems and bad habits like anyone else. But the experience very strongly woke me up and gave me the power to transform myself at incredible speed. Why? The profound power of the source of my experience absolutely convinced me that there is a truth and this truth is love.

I received tremendous energy from the source of my experience—God—and this energy gave me the power to transform myself. Before I was not able to change myself because I did not know the truth and thereby I was lost. But from my experience I learned the deep nature of love and with the power of this I was able to change. This is what Ring calls "the spiritual catalyst" that propelled me to change by the power of the Light.[47]

This authentic response to the ultimate reality tells us something about its nature. These significant life-changes by people who have near-death experiences are evidence of its reality. There is really something 'out there' that is ultimately true, and the nature of this reality is love. The dynamic of the life-changes comes from a force of the universe that inspires movement on a foundation of truth. This truth—the most powerful force in the universe—is love.

The fact that in this world we can become like God also means that heaven is not only 'out there,' but right here in this world. The chance to love is here right now. This was also a profound lesson from my experience, that I had had the chance to love, but this chance was lost because I did not know that it is all love.

One person who truly understood this and manifested compassion in our world was Mother Theresa. When visiting her tomb in Calcutta, India, I was deeply touched by the text from the Bible next to her name: "Love each other as I have loved you."

Reading this, I cried, remembering what a powerful manifestation of the deep meaning of these words her life had been. The light shone through her into this world, taking away the pain of those who suffered the most. She was a true saint, reflecting pure light into this world.

She was the embodiment of the words: "*What is not given is lost*," and for me, these words are the closest that we can get to truly understanding the profound nature of the light in this dimension. I have not come across a better interpretation that captures the powerful nature of the purpose of the essence of life. If more of us knew the true meaning of the light, more would try to live as a manifestation of it in this world. Mother Theresa truly lived the words of the Bible, "Let us love, not in words or speech, but in truth and action...for God is greater than our hearts."[48]

One way that we can all reach towards that which is greater than our hearts, is by learning the Golden Rule and growing into a deeper understanding of its profound meaning. This is the profound meaning that the Bible explains by telling us that whoever lives in love—lives in God.[49] We can all begin to live in the light of God by implementing a deeper understanding of the Golden Rule in our lives. This begins with self-love which is then expanded onto the world around us. The love that we see in ourselves and our family now manifests in others. We see beyond our physical world into the essence of love, or we see the world from our essence of love.

This is what Plato told us that, being enlightened, we can see through the imperfect earthly manifestation into the eternal essence that lies beneath it.[50] What this means is that when we see each other's true nature, we see through the earthly form and into the universal essence of love. Through seeing what is higher in each of us, we can lift each other up to reach the light within us all.

In this way, we see each other's higher self, or potential, instead of looking for the negation that pulls someone down. Our personalities and patterns are only the surface, and underneath we are all souls with a deep longing to be united through love. Love is our true nature and the deep desire in all human beings. When we see past and beyond each other's imperfect manifestations, we see each other's soul and true identity. Now, we can begin to meet other people with genuine respect in alignment with the Golden Rule.

God is love and this is how we see God in each other. This is also what Elaine Pagels explains in *Beyond Belief*: the true message of the Gnostic interpretation of Christianity is to "encourage and sustain the recognition of the light within us all."[51] The eternal essence that Plato wants us to see is the light within us all. Science tells us that everything is energy made of light, and the near-death experience confirms what religion already knows that this light is love.

This is also how I met my wife. Having searched 32 years of my life, our first encounter was a hug that lasted for an hour and fifteen minutes. We instantly both knew and through our openness in this moment, we were able to recognize each other's light by seeing beyond the earthly manifestations and into our true nature which was one—one soul in two bodies.

The light is our true nature and we all have the same nature—we are love. Kenneth Ring confirms this by telling us that, "The absolute and unconditional love of the Light reveals the essence of the individual's true self."[52] We already have it in us, so there is no need to go look for it, because it is already there inside. Our true nature is an infinite and unending source of love.

If we do not feel connected to ourselves, it is because we are blocking the natural flow of love. For me, the pain of the life-review was the realization that I had been separated from Love—my true nature. Thereby, I had been separated from God and being separated from my true nature was the separation from my-self. It was this separation, which turned into an emptiness that made me go against my true nature.

So, it all starts with self-love, and this self-love comes from our true nature. Having an identity—knowing who we are—is the foundation of self-love because our true nature is love. Therefore, when we know who we are, we naturally feel good about ourselves because our essence is a natural flow of love and joy.

Knowing who we are also gives us freedom from victimization because no one can tell us who to *be* when we know who we *are*. Being light as our true nature we are the essence of the universe and from this essence we are free. As light we are in total alignment with the center of the whole universe and in this alignment we are one with God.

This alignment with God also means that we can begin to create and manifest as co-creators with God. In the ancient Yogi tradition of India it has been known for thousands of years that the source of creation is light. By understanding the source of creation and knowing that we can manifest or alter the light, we take control of our part in the creation process of the universe.

The Yogis explain that the *law of miracles* can be used by any human being who has realized that the essence of creation is light. Therefore, "Any man [or woman] of divine realization could perform miracles, because he [or she] understands the subtle laws of creation."[53] In this way, the Yogi Master is able to apply this "divine knowledge" to the act of creation by projecting the light particles into manifestation.

Even science agrees with this today, where the smallest particle in our physical world is the photon, which is light. The way that the *law of attraction* works, according to science, is that through the photons "particles influence each other by exchanging these smallest bundles of light."[54] The light works as a "messenger-particle" that transmits a message to the particles in our universe. The more light that is exchanged, the more force is created and thereby the stronger the attraction.

The study of consciousness explains that the quantum field is in fact consciousness. And these fields of consciousness are connected to the light because the mind acts as a matrix for the light—mind is the light.[55] Through this we have finally placed consciousness—or true nature—at the center of creation. By using our mind to manifest light particles through our thoughts we become co-creators of the universe.

Hereby, co-creation with God becomes the thinking like God—naturally thinking positive and loving thoughts—from the source of our true nature. What we focus our attention on will grow, and this is why positive thinking creates a positive life for us and our environment. We manifest what we think by feeding the object of our projection energy. This is just like a plant; if we feed it water, it will grow. This basic principle works on everything in the universe because everything is energy.

By knowing who we are, we also know who God is because our true nature is one with God. This is how we live in God by aligning ourselves with the light inside of us. And by seeing the light within all of humanity and all of life, we are able to manifest God in this dimension, whereby we are truly able to live *in* God.

Reconcile

After my experience, one of the first actions I did was write down a list of all the people that I could remember having hurt in my life.

My negative life-review had impacted me so strongly that my remorse pushed me to ask forgiveness. I felt a newfound compassion for all human beings, and I felt it was important to express this compassion. As I looked up people such as old friends and ex-girlfriends one by one, I realized that it was an expression of love to acknowledge their pain and say I was sorry for causing it.

I experienced the inner workings of the Golden Rule by entering the pain of others and restoring the balance through healing. This process made me see through myself and the people on my list into the essence of the deepest level of life. By acknowledging the pain of life, it made life more real for me, and also more real for them. It felt as intense as if I were connecting to the heart of life.

I especially remember one person that I had hurt before my awakening. He had been a close friend but a girl had come between us, and being weak and selfish, I had hurt him. I wanted to say that I was sorry, but I almost did not have the courage to do so. Not only was I ashamed, but I was afraid that he might still be so angry that he would hit me.

Finally, I 'coincidentally' bumped into him. I knew that this was the chance to seize the moment. I had a lot of fear facing him, but I knew what was right, so I broke through the amour of ice. I said his name, looked him in the eye, and said: "What happened between us...for that I am truly sorry. I am deeply sorry and it has been with me ever since."

It was a great moment. The ice melted and everything became warm again. We hugged with tears in our eyes. As I had been sad, so he had also been sad, and by healing my scar I healed his as well. As both our scars were interconnected, one scar dissolved the other. In this moment I truly felt how my repentance brought reconciliation.

If we look into the meaning of repentance this experience is reflected. In Greek we find that to repent means a "change of mind or heart" or simply to "change one's mind."[56] By changing our mind, we change our lives. When repentance meets sin, things are restored back to its balance. As we saw earlier, sin is what turns consciousness away from truth. Through repentance, we change the direction of our mind and turn our consciousness back towards truth again. Thereby we are forgiven by God, because sin—the false consciousness—is no more.

Repentance equalizes sin without punishment, because the target is truth. The near-death experience tells us that the light is truth and love. One of the most important lessons that we can learn from the near-death experience is that, "The Light does not judge," it only loves.[57] In the same way, it is not God that does the punishment because God is love. It is the experience of having turned our consciousness away from truth, and thereby being separated from God that is painful. It is the pain of being separate from God, the truth, which is the 'punishment.'

In this way, we repent by turning our consciousness back towards truth, and that is all that is needed. We are not here to be punished but to learn. The pain of being separated from truth is in itself punishment enough, and as soon as the lesson is learned there is no longer need for an angry teacher. The Bible tells us that "God was reconciling the world (to himself in Christ), not counting men's sins against them."[58] And Jesus tells us that "whatever you bind on earth will be bound in heaven, and whatever you loose on earth will be loosed in heaven."[59]

This is what we learn from the near-death experience, that the light does not count our sins. And by forgiving and being forgiven we are untying the knots that keep us separate from our true nature. In this way we can heal the scars in us, in people around us, and in the whole world. If we look deeply into the cause of suffering and misery in our world, we can see that much of it comes from pain. The pain is so heavy in many of us that it keeps us trapped, and thereby, forgiving instead of punishing is truly the best way out of the pain.

Not counting our sins also means that we have to balance our judgment. Being able to discriminate is important, but judging too much, too hard, and too often, takes us away from love. We use our logic to discriminate, which is good, but at the same time we use our labels of wrong and right to judge each other endlessly.

As we looked at earlier, one way to do this is to see sin as ignorance instead of evil. This was what Kierkegaard did in reminding us that Adam was innocent. To punish him and every man and woman to follow, would be like punishing a toddler for falling down.

Parents who punish their child for its innocence are themselves immature, because when we punish each other with the intention to cause harm, the others can neither see nor understand what they have done wrong. In ignorance, no one can see the reason for their punishment. And so starts the circle of violence and revenge that we see in the world because we cannot remove hatred with hatred, and we cannot remove darkness with darkness.

The problem with punishment is that it causes self-hatred. By punishing innocent children we are saying they are not good enough— something is wrong with them. If we make such children believe they deserve the punishment, we make them feel ashamed of themselves. Both self-hatred and shame leads to self-destruction through feeling pain.

As a society, we have to ask ourselves where depression and self-hatred come from. With teenagers killing themselves, and many adults feeling alienated and empty, something is wrong. Where does this self-destruction come from?

In my view, a qualified guess is our doctrine of punishment. From ancient times, we have created a social doctrine of reward and punishment. This is what we call the stick and carrot. In one hand, authority holds a stick and in the other a carrot, so we are forced to run in fear towards that thing we desire. Try for a moment to imagine how this must feel to an innocent child that is born into our world.

Surely, our children need guidance but the question is what should this guidance be founded on? The near-death experience tells us that love should be the foundation instead of our conditioning of reward and punishment.

Also William Desmond explains that forgiveness is beyond morality—a transmoral forgiveness—not based on an eye for an eye, but beyond "self and other" and beyond wrong and right in a more ultimate sense.[60] Transmoral forgiveness separates our actions from who we really are and greets us as the non-judgmental light.

A profound example of transmoral forgiveness that was sadly made into a media event in 2006 was the Amish school shooting in Pennsylvania. A lost and tormented soul entered a small schoolhouse, and after separating out ten very young girls he shot them, killing six, and then himself when the police came. This horrible crime, difficult to comprehend, illustrates what it actually means to be disconnected from the true nature of life.

Yet this community showed the rest of the world how to react. Instead of anger and revenge, the Amish community responded with understanding and forgiveness. Not only did the community forgive, but the community attended the funeral of the man who killed their children. Watching these events on TV, I was touched deeply by the heartfelt response of forgiveness to this tragic event. If only the world and our governments could contain this kind of forgiveness in their hearts, then maybe our world could begin to change for the better.

The Balance

"O Lord, if I worship you out of fear of hell,
burn me in hell.

If I worship you in the hope of paradise,
forbid it to me.

And if I worship you for your own sake,
Do not deprive me of your eternal beauty.[61]

Saint of Islam, Rabi´a Adawiya, a central female figure in the Sufi tradition in the eight century, shows us the right balance in this poem, surrendering to the middle between the two extremes of fear and desire. The words are about worship, but they also talk about the right relationship to life. Her words demonstrate that the stick and carrot doctrine is not a new phenomenon, and that domination through fear and seduction has followed humanity through history.

Fear is probably the oldest form of control known to humans. We naturally carry a fear of the dark within us and most of us are naturally afraid of dying. When taken advantage of this, fear can be used to control us. This is how religion, government, and all levels of power have dominated humans for centuries.

Here I would like to say that the near-death experience takes away the deep rooted fear of dying through the insight that death is not the end. However, if someone is not convinced of this, it is also possible to be free of the fear by recognizing its nature. If we are afraid of the dark it is mostly because our eyes have not been adjusted to it, and thereby, we are unable to see. But if we look closely, we will see that there are many things in the dark that we are afraid of, but there is only *one* fear. By internalizing this insight about the nature of fear, we can overcome it.

The next step is to free ourselves from being a victim of fear by stopping the manifestation of fear in our lives. Like we saw before, when we feed something energy it will grow. By sending photons of light towards our fear, or what we do not want, we make it grow in the same way we make a plant grow by feeding it water. Being mindful of this sub-conscious process will liberate us from the manifestation of fear in our lives.

This also works with desire and any kind of attachment or aversion. As we went through in chapter six, a mindful and balanced mind can steer clear of falling into extremes. Through meditation or the practice of mindfulness, we can see our sub-conscious patterns of attachment and aversion, and by becoming aware of these patterns we can choose not to bite on the hook. This is the key point of Adawiya's poem, to find the right balance between the two extremes. In the middle is our true nature as the foundation that frees us to see life as it really is.

The Sufi tradition also teaches us that we need to find the balance between continuance and disappearance—the balance between the physical and spiritual world, the body and the soul, or matter and energy. As humans we are in a constant dynamic between the opposites of what is continuing and what is disappearing.

Desmond explains that,

> We have neither the bliss of the beast's ignorance nor the blessedness of the god's gnosis [knowledge]...We know we do not know the absolute truth, yet we know, and hence are not cut off from, the truth we clearly do not possess. We often are split creatures, torn in two between our dark doubt and a thirst for truth that cannot be slaked.[62]

Not only are we spilt between these two extremes, but everything is also made more complex through the fact that, "Different modes of being true are true in relation to the different senses of being."[63] After my experience, I found myself in this complex construct, split into extremes. Before I had only known one reality—our physical world, and now through my experience I saw another reality. This was what created a split in me trying to find out which reality was the real one. Being ruled by logic and the forced choice of either/or, I had to make a choice and this forced choice was what created the split in me. Coming back to myself, I first had to accept that both realities were real and thereby I chose a both/and instead of the either/or.

I found the logic that helped me solve the paradox in the East. Here in Buddhism the two extremes are characterized as relative and absolute truth. These two extremes of truth that seem to be separate are not separate but two sides of the same truth. The absolute truth is the inconceivable and indescribable truth that would be the same ultimate reality that the near-death experiencer enters.

This non-conceptual absolute truth is being in itself and it can be reached through meditation. The relative truth is our conceptual understanding of the absolute truth. Relative truths are the names and labels that we put on the absolute truth, or we could say that these are our interpretations of the absolute truth. It is the difference between the truth as perceived and the truth itself.

In this way there can be many relative truths as reflections of the absolute truth. One example is the many different religions that all point towards the same absolute truth. What is important in this view of the truth is that the relative truths are not false because they are still perceptions of the truth, whereby they reflect the absolute truth. The relative truths contain parts of the truth as the surface of the absolute truth, which only goes deeper into the essence of truth. When we fight over relative truths it is not because one relative truth is untrue, it is because we forget that our relative truth is only relative and not absolute.

The problem in the way that we have constructed Western thought is that we tend to reject duality. If there can be only one truth in a multi-dimensional world, and the logic of our mind demands that we only pick one, then we are forced to reject the other as untrue (either/or). This is why I prefer duality and the logic of both/and.

The difference in this view is that it does not force us into extremes. Both the relative truth and the absolute truth are true—a new form of logic that opens up our view of the world. In this duality there is room for both truths because they are complementary, since we need the relative truth to get to the absolute truth. And rather than rejecting one truth, duality lets us accept the two truths and find the balance between them.

Desmond tells us that, "Truth is a correspondence between the 'in here' and the 'out there'."[64] In other words, truth is the right balance between the relative and absolute—the subjective and objective. There needs to be balance between the absolute truth and the relative truths. This balance is described in Buddhism as a bird that needs two wings to fly. Each wing needs to be equally strong and in harmony with the other for the bird to fly, and only when in perfect balance can the bird fly towards the absolute in the skies above.

Instead of relative and absolute truth being in conflict, they must work together to create harmony through balance. When the Truth is found in the balance between the two, rather than in the extreme of opposites, then it makes it possible for the two to meet—to become one. This truth is found in the diplomatic balance that aims at uniting rather than separating the two, where one is put above the other as the true and the other is suppressed as false. By not condemning one through the other's victory, a balance between the two can be found where both are treated with equal respect.

Now, this balance is not blind to the truth—it aims for the truth through oneness rather than through the extreme that suppresses its opposite. By aiming at the truth without forgetting that our aim is only a relative truth and not *the* absolute Truth, we are able to leave room for the truths of others. This is a balanced search for Truth that permits "the other" to live instead of being crucified by the truth. Through this understanding of truth it is much easier to arrive at a deeper understanding of the Golden Rule, which leaves room for all of us to live in love and respect.

This is also why Buddhism places less emphasis on right and wrong, but concentrates on the concepts of wholesome and unwholesome to steer away from the judgment. In the same way, to the ancient Greeks, truth had a different meaning than our view on it today. They interpreted *truthful* as meaning, "realizing itself," or "coming to fulfillment."[65] This also fits with the Greek understanding of *perfection*, which is translated as "fulfillment," or "completion."[66]

Through this different view on the truth we are able to change our perspective on the world we live in. This is a view where the aggressive black/white suppression of what is "wrong" is opened up to a world view that is more accepting through being able to see the multi-layered color scheme of whole world. If the goal is not to be "right," but instead to be *fulfilled* then there is less reason to punish or kill others who do not think like us. And if our personal goal is to be fulfilled, rather than being "perfect," then we can realize ourselves through the surrender to the true nature of reality. When we cannot force reality—we have to accept reality—and surrender to it.

Chapter Ten

The World

After my personal life-review, my near-death experience took me through all the pain in our world. In this view of the world I saw all the war and conflict, and all the poor and suffering people in it. Not only did I see it, I also felt all the pain of the world; I felt the torment of all the people suffering due to war and poverty. All this misery was too much for my heart to bear.

Looking at all this suffering from the light is truly painful. Imagine all the anguish in our world gathered in one enormous concentration of energy in pain. This was what I felt. The profound and unlimited love that lies at the essence of life is so far from the suffering and conflict we see in our world. Having experienced the light, I try to imagine how children see our world and how painful it must be for them to enter into it. I truly wish that instead of adapting the children to our world that we could adapt to their world by creating a secure place of peace and harmony.

An old friend of mine, my brother Chief Sonne Reyna, used to say that, "Love is the only truth—everything else is politics." On the complex world stage of geo-politics, I do not seek to take sides because I do not believe divisive politics is the answer. But I do believe that instead of fighting and killing each other, we need to work together and co-operate in solving the challenges that we are facing as one human family. Everything is connected in our universe, and therefore, we have to evolve from us and them to the understanding of we in order to reach the love behind our politics.

There is an old Mayan saying that, "I am the other you"—you and I are one—we are interconnected. There is no enemy because as Nobel Price winner, Orham Pamuk tells us: "We are the other." This is the essence of the Golden Rule; what ever we do to our neighbor we do to ourselves because *we are the other*.

The world we live in today seems far from this understanding. The beginning of the new millennium has shown clear signs of aggressive reactions from extremes on both sides. There is a clear moral problem with the direction we have taken during this new beginning. The aggressive right has clearly broken the Golden Rule and this break is causing imbalance in our world through destabilization.

This is a historical problem that we have had for thousands of years. If we did not know it already, then, at least the 20th century has clearly shown us the suffering of war through two World Wars and nearly a third. War is the most painful and senseless activity we can do as humans and we find no other creature in nature as destructive as us. Former U.N. Secretary-General, Kofi Annan, told us that, "In war *all* are losers."

This is ultimately true. The victims of war lose their lives but we as humanity lose part of our soul. Killing another human—*taking* the life from another human being—is the ultimate disrespect, and thereby, in direct conflict with the Golden Rule. As I said in chapter eight, I can only imagine what it must be like to go through a life-review after having killed another human being.

The ignorance of the immense disrespect or hate that brings someone to kill another person will dissolve painfully in the true nature of the light. Peter Fenwick puts it like this: "Imagine someone you dislike. Now try to imagine yourself filled with the kind of universal love that so often suffuses people in the near-death experience. In this emotional state it must be very hard to hate your enemy."[1]

In fact, I would say that it is absolutely impossible. You cannot hate nor have hard feelings there because the true nature of reality is unimaginably infinite love. Any hate or negative feeling is completely dissolved in it, and then, when we experience that everything is connected, our actions of killing another will be like we were killing ourselves. What we do to others we truly do to ourselves. This is the Golden Rule—the law of the universe that we cannot escape.

However, looking at the world, it clearly seems that many of us are ignorant of this truth. We live inside Plato's dark cave, as prisoners captured in the physical world and only able to see the shadows cast against the wall. Inside the cave, we compete in measuring the shadows, argue over who owns them and in fear we fight to hold on to them.

In this darkness, many of us have no time to stop and think about what is really going on around us; why are we in such a hurry? One guess could be that for some of us with only one life to live, we have to hurry to get everything here and now. It is clear that with the knowledge of life after death, life has a longer perspective than the short one we see in this day and age in the Western world.

In addition, the darkness inside the cave scares us. We think that we are free, but if we truly were, we would not be so scared. Thus, survival of the fittest becomes the only science of social law because we live in fear of our own survival. But when life is eternal and God truly loves us, then this is really all just shadows of illusion.

It is true that from a strictly spiritual or absolute point of view, the mature way to stop the fighting is to stop feeding it energy. By not feeding the conflict energy, we stop adding to the bad karma. However, from a relative point of view I believe that we cannot simply watch and say nothing while people are being killed. As people of the world living *in* the world, we cannot simply disconnect from it and passively look on while others are suffering.

Something has to be said and something has to be done, in order for us to arrive at a mature level of understanding where we are able to stop the fighting. Being honest, I will have to be humble and admit that the human game of politics is extremely complex. But still, I feel compelled to speak out, and therefore, I would like to take a look at some of the problems that we are facing right now and suggest some solutions based on my personal observations. It is my hope that rather than only adding to the conflict, some of my observations may cast light from outside the cave on to the shadows inside.

The Shadow Game

As a teenager, I went to senior high school in Colorado, U.S.A. One thing that has stayed with me from this time of my life was the first party I attended a few weeks after I had arrived. Even though as a kid I had been involved in fighting before, this event surprised me deeply to the extent that it could be called a culture shock. At some point during this party everyone there had gathered up into a big circle and I noticed that there was a lot of shouting. When I went to see what was going on, I saw that in the middle of the circle, an overweight student was being beaten while everyone cheered.

By instinct I went into the circle and split the one-sided fight up, only to find myself as the new target of the beating. My shock was not so much that the angry bully wanted to beat me up instead, but that the crowd turned against me to cheer him on in doing so. I was able to defend myself, but still the reaction from the crowd was a shock to me.

I have since thought a lot about crowd behavior. What makes a crowd go blind?

One of the biggest crowd controllers is organized religion. Even though the Catholic Church in 1953 officially renounced their position that "No salvation [exists] outside the Church,"[2] many of our problems today certainly seem to originate from the fundamental belief that, "I am the way and the truth and the life. No one comes to the Father except through me."[3]

Polls show that 36 percent of Americans believe that the Bible is the word of God and is to be taken literally.[4] And on top of this it is evident that the U.S. has problems with religious groups who forget to keep Caesar and God separate. According to exit polls in the 2004 re-election, 79 percent of 26 million Evangelical Christians voted for George W. Bush.[5] Polls also show that 71 percent from this group of devoted believers supported the war in Iraq.[6] Would Jesus really have supported the war in Iraq?

The Christian religion was born out of conflict in a time of great turmoil. The early Church quickly transformed into a powerful institution as it merged with the Roman Empire to become the state religion. Historian Erik Peterson explains that in this process many Christians came to associate God with the Emperor, Jesus with the Bishop, and the Holy Spirit with the people.[7] This was why in the 17th century when Descartes separated the body from the soul, he also separated the state from the Church.

The war in Iraq is sold as a religious war. President Bush strategically uses the words "God" and "good and evil" in his rhetoric when speaking directly to his voters on the Christian right, and he even uses the word "crusade" to define his "war on terror." Ultimately, we cannot separate culture from religion and if we look closely, we can see that the pre-emptive push for democracy comes from an underlying idea of conversion that is ingrained in our colonial reasoning.

Now some people, especially atheists, blame God—or the belief in God—for the existence of fundamentalism. These days we can find this view with Richard Dawkins, the author of *The God Delusion*. While I do agree that organized religion does cause certain serious problems related to fundamentalism, I do not believe that it is God who is the source of this problem.

When we kill each other over who is right, or whose God is the true God, it is a misunderstanding—a spiritual immature view—that is to blame. It is the literal interpretation and misconception of God that does the killing—not God 'himself.' It is not the light of God, but our stubborn ignorance that is the cause of the violence.

One example of this is the words of Jesus in Matthew 10:34, "I did not come to bring peace, but a sword," which have been (and are still!) used as an argument for war and killing in the name of Christ. These words, however, are taken out of context, because—"For I have come to.."—Jesus is not talking about war here, but about the truth as a sword dividing family members apart. If we cannot see this clearly in Matthew, we can look in Luke 12:51, where we can see that the metaphor of the "sword" is replace by the word "division." It is this kind of literal interpretation that leads us into fundamental views, when we use the words of Jesus to justify our political actions.

To show us where it is that we have gone wrong, I will let my friend, Professor Robert Sellers, explain it from his own experience. Rob was an Evangelical missionary during his younger days, and has transformed Plato's cave allegory into what he learned about conversion while spreading the 'good news' in Indonesia.

He says that the ones who have found their own way out of the darkness of the cave, are "ecstatic" over their own salvation and in this inflated state over having seen the light, they rush to tell everyone else out of compassion. The problem, however, is that there might be more than one exit, and so, Rob asks:

> Are we really in a position to speak with certainty about pathways we ourselves have never walked? Or, rather, is it the case that all we *can* do is to testify with passion about the *one* path we *have* traveled— and the light we *have* seen?[8]

Plato himself told us that having lived in darkness for all of our lives and then suddenly coming out of the cave to see the sun for the very first time, it takes time for our eyes to adapt to the light. The sun is too bright as the absolute truth is inconceivable and indescribable, whereby our discovery has us "ecstatic" but in this state also blinded.

Therefore, as in Plato's story, the right way to help the others in the cave becomes the biggest challenge. This is a problem that I know very well after actually having seen the light outside the cave. Personally, as an Aries, I am naturally enthusiastic and I will admit that even as I write this book the challenge of how to communicate the light is big.

To describe this, Rob tells us that "some Christians—having 'seen the light'—act as if they can 'see' perfectly." Believing so strongly in the light that they have seen that they are willing to kill or let others die for their interpretation of the light is ignorance. The intention of wanting to show others '*the*' light might be good, but the light is too bright for our eyes, and therefore, we should all approach others "with humility rather than arrogance."[9]

Here again it makes sense to mention Tillich's characterization of God beyond God, as the ground of being that underlies all our concepts and images. By understanding that the Bible, like any religion, can be understood in many other ways than our particular interpretation of it, we have a good starting point from where we can begin to practice the Golden Rule.

The near-death experience gives testimony of a universal spiritual orientation that sees the underlying nature of the light as a "pure religion" beyond religion—a unified essence of oneness. Kenneth Ring tells us that,

> The strongest evidence of NDErs' universalistically spiritual orientation...is their belief in the underlying unity of all religions and their desire for a universal religious faith that will transcend the historical divisiveness of the world's great religions.[10]

It is not only in religion that we find fundamentalism, it is also alive and well in the form of imperialism. Even today in the third millennium, America as an Empire does not hold back the implementation of its national interests through foreign policies that go against its internal moral foundation.

In 1910, French advocate of colonialism, Jules Harmand said about *moral superiority* that, "Our dignity rests on that quality, and it underlies our right to direct the rest of humanity. Material power is nothing but a means to that end."[11]

What this tells us is that the left over of our colonial mind believes that material power equals moral superiority. This, however, is a mistake because moral authority is not a power-game. It is founded on truth and the effect of this cause can be seen directly through one's actions. Today probably the best case to show us where we are is the Iraq war, which clearly shows us how blind and ignorant we are within our cave.

Jim Garrison, founder of the State of the World Forum, explains how America has changed from republic into empire:

> America has made the transition from republic to empire. It is no longer what it was. It was founded to become a beacon of light unto the nations, a democratic and egalitarian haven to which those seeking freedom could come. It has now become an unrivalled

empire among the nations, exercising dominion over them. How it behaves and what it represents have fundamentally changed. It used to represent freedom. Now it represents power.[12]

Garrison also tells us that the definition of empire is the exercise of control over other nations, and while America still remains a republic within its borders, it has now become an empire in its interaction with the rest of the world. This does not only show itself through pre-emptive war but also in the manner that the present government conveniently turns its back on international agreements and institutions because it prefers the freedom to dictate its own self-interest.

In one of his last speeches, Kofi Annan directed his words at the U.S.A. by saying that playing by the rules "can sometimes be inconvenient. But ultimately what matters is not inconvenience—it is doing the right thing."[13]

If the U.S. does not set the moral standard by playing by the rules better than anyone else, it will loose its moral authority. Here I believe that it is wise to remember that empires do not last. And in remembering this, maybe some hard line American's on the far right should think about how they would feel about China's future 'liberations' of weaker states as it emerges as a new superpower. The coming next empire will most likely learn to play the game from our actions today, so how we act now will have implications for tomorrow.

To have a moral authority obligates one to set the moral direction of the future. In doing so, it is vital that we do not lie to ourselves, but instead reflect on our true intentions *and* the consequences of our actions. This was clearly not done in the case of the war in Iraq, and therefore the war was lost from the beginning. Bad intentions where exposed through lies, and ignorance has caused the deaths of thousands of innocent people. Even the world's greatest military power cannot escape Truth—Truth confronts you no matter how much power you have.

Here the neo-conservatives have a clear flaw in their reasoning. They want to impose freedom and democracy on to the world, but do not want the U.N. or any body else to question the manner in which they carry out their plan for the world and the rest of us. On one hand they promote the ideal of democracy but on the other they themselves do not want to listen to the world community. If they do not get their way, they simply go solo and force their views on to the rest of the world, because as Richard Perle tells us: "There has to be an advantage to being a superpower."[14]

Now, I should say that before my experience I was far more right than left, so I do understand our reasons for believing that war is the right means to change the world. In 1991, I supported the first Gulf War to stop the aggression of Saddam, but also underneath I feared an 'evil' danger in our world. So, I do not mean to point fingers at Bush or the majority of American's that believed the war was just in the beginning. I actually have compassion and do understand where the fear and the anger come from.

However, I wish to look at where we went wrong in the hope that we can learn from our mistakes, and in this case I think that it is clearly a question of faulty logic. The so-called "struggle between good and evil" combined with the "either you are with us, or you are with the terrorists" philosophy is really a problematic view of the world.

Throughout history again and again, warmongers have made us believe that through war we can achieve peace. By making us afraid, this logic makes us fight against our fears, thus actually manifesting them. The U.S. is at war with its own shadow because it sees danger everywhere, whereby America is manifesting its own fear in the world. Aggression through pre-emption comes from the fear of losing control and so in the desire to restore control, danger is attributed to put an issue above dispute. In this way, the fear manifests itself and becomes a self-fulfilling prophecy.

Through this trick, the Church and the Western mind has been contaminated with destruction and conflict for ages. In this logic, which has imperialistic aggression built in to it, there is no room for other alternatives. Thus, due to black/white, either/or thinking we are headed straight into conflict—and even worse, corruption of the truth.

German philosopher, Martin Heidegger explained that the Latin word *falsum* for false has created a "linguistic confusion" that has lead us to an alienation from truth. To the Greeks there was no word for false, but instead the equivalent meaning would be "to bring to ruin" or "to make unsteady." In Heidegger's words the Latin word "false" has become a "deception," and he tells us that this deception of the Latin understanding of false leads to the "trick" of creating true as its opposite.[15]

In his book on Heidegger, Victor Farías writes that, "For the development of the Latin *falsum*, the link to the 'imperium' and the Imperial was essential, that is, the link to what the others dismiss." Thereby, the influence of the Roman Empire through the Latin understanding of the word false "was a mediating factor in a degeneration that in modern times has encroached upon the entire world, and its influence has lead to the decline of the essence of truth."[16]

Sociologist and thinker Zygmunt Bauman sees this fight over who is right as a primal and primitive instinct. He explains how this primitive instinct makes each side fight the difference of the other in the name of their own purity.[17] What it boils down to is that in "us and them," "they" scare us because of their otherness and this difference leads us to fight them in the name of our purity. As we fight purity in ourselves, we also fight it in others, and so we fight our own shadow because we are afraid of it.

In *Purity and Danger,* Mary Douglas takes this point further by explaining that the paradox in the search for purity is that it forces us into logical categories of non-contradiction. But since experience and absolute reality cannot fit into boxes, "those who make the attempt find themselves led into contradiction."[18]

This is how our either/or logic leads us into contradiction and thereby tricks us into conflict. At the same time, within this conflict we also find our resistance to change. Douglas tells us that because purity is "the enemy of change, of ambiguity and compromise. Most of us indeed would feel safer if our experience could be hard-set and fixed in form."[19]

Now, when we take this faulty logic and mix it with the demonization of our 'enemies' it gets even worse, because it leads us into blind vengeance. A post-9/11 poll done by *Religion & Ethics Newsweekly* found that 61 percent of Americans believe that "evil in the world" is the biggest threat.[20] Thereby, it seems that all the evil empire talk has truly made people believe in an "axis of evil." Or the world does actually look evil to many religious Americans, since 59 percent believe that the End Time prophecies in the *Book of Revelation* will come true.[21]

Then, when living in an evil world, 'of course,' we need an angry God to punish the evildoers. To confirm this, polls show that 31 percent of Americans believe in an Authoritarian God that "is angry at sin and can punish the unfaithful or ungodly." Of these people, nearly a third of the population in America, 63 percent believe that the government should increase military spending, and 76 percent that the government should expand authority to fight terrorism. Also, 63 percent of these followers of an angry God believe that the war in Iraq is justified.[22]

Here again, I believe that we should ask ourselves: What sort of God is this? If this is an angry and vengeful God from the Old Testament who lives in a world with a pending judgment day, then truly the whole world might as well go blind. If the true nature of humanity is inherent evil, then yes: "Do on to others before they do on to you." But how can we ever trust each other and build a lasting peace if this is how we think?

Most of us (hopefully the rest) know that even when we are angry, this is not the case. God is love and what makes him angry is our own anger—by seeing red we paint the world red. If we believe in an angry God that must confront evil in the world by fighting pre-emptive wars, then we have made God pro war—a God of war. And then the question we need to ask ourselves is; whether this active aggression comes from God or from us?

Douglas points back to the lectures of Hebrew scholar Robertson Smith in 1891, before he was dismissed for heresy. Back then, Smith said that the Old Testament has in it "a false philosophy of Revelation," where the demons are the primitive elements to be rejected. He explained that even though we in religion may find at times that God is angry, this is "only in times of social dissolution."[23]

The Old Testament is set in a very specific time in history. The years of wandering in the desert after the exodus, was indeed a time of social dissolution for the people of Israel. The times may indeed have demanded that Moses be hard on his people, but this time in history does not make God angry at all times till the end of time (unless we truly want the end of time).

Robertson Smith explained further that,

> However true it is that savage man feels himself to be environed by innumerable dangers which he does not understand and so personifies as invisible or mysterious enemies of more than human power, it is not true that the attempt to appease these powers is the foundation of religion.[24]

The false philosophy of anger within the Christian tradition has not evolved to adapt to the world we live in today. Just by comparing the Old Testament with the New Testament, we can clearly see that Jesus is living in another time. The words of Jesus are difficult to follow if we all let our anger out by returning 'evil' for 'evil.' Here we should remember that Jesus lived in a turbulent time of Roman occupation, but instead of creating an uprising he transformed the Roman Empire from within. So, maybe Jesus tells us to turn the other cheek, not only to pacify us but also to make us see *first* before we go blind—to think before we act.

An old poem by Lanza del Vasto explains to us how we not only go blind by returning evil for evil, but also forge our own chains of imprisonment:

> If you return evil for evil, you do not undo the damage, you only strengthen it. How can you label good, the evil that you perpetrate? If you kill the murderer to punish him, you still have not brought the victim back to life. Instead there are two deaths, not one, and two murderers, he and you... Violence is a chain. Anyone who tries to free himself through violence ends up forging his own chain.[25]

Revenge and punishment do not set our souls free or create a better world for our children. They make us slaves to anger and hatred. Compassion and forgiveness are the ways out of the pattern of reaction that keeps our true nature imprisoned. The use of aggression and war is not a noble cause—working to sustain the Golden Rule is. Respect for life, not destruction of it through war, is what is truly noble in the light of God.

In our ignorant eagerness to do the opposite of 'evil,' it seems evident we are seeing our world upside down. By using the trick label "evil" we say that *up is down* and *black is white*. But evil is ignorance—no one does evil with full enlightened intent. Even the worst example of evil is ignorance, since also Hitler used the words: "Gott ist mit uns"— God is with us.

So, then how do we define evil (if we must)? And how do we see our world right side up? To answer this I will use James Newton Poling's definition of evil:

> Evil is the abuse of power in personal, social, and religious forms that destroys bodies and spirits. Evil is an abuse of power because the power of life comes from God, and all power should be used for good. Whenever power is used to destroy the bodies and spirits of God's creation, there is evil.[26]

We have seen plenty of abuse of power that has led us into the massive conflict we are in today. When we allow the killing of innocent people by believing *our* end is justifying our means, we are forgetting that this power comes from God alone. Telling ourselves that God is on our side and that God would permit the killing of the innocent is only a game of shadows inside our dark cave.

Our perception of evil has an aggressive rejection within due to our fear of it, while the perception of ignorance has a compassionate rejection within. No matter how much we wish to be free of 'evil,' we cannot fight ingnorance with ingnorance because we unable to see clearly in our fear and anger.

It is not God that leads us to these actions, but our own fear of the darkness. Because we are afraid of the dark, we fear our own shadow whereby we label it "evil." This is also how Douglas finishes her argument. It is our fear of evil which makes us kill in the name of purity, and this fear kills others because of our own fear of dying. The only way to overcome this fear is a voluntary embrace of death that is "a protection, not against death but against madness."[27]

In *The Fear of Freedom* Erich Fromm explains that our fear makes us powerless, and that it is this powerlessness that makes us destroy our shadow: "The destruction of the world is the last, almost desperate attempt to save myself from being crushed by it."[28] And he tells us that,

> If there is no objective "reason" for the expression of destructiveness, we call the person mentally or emotional sick (although the person himself will usually build up some sort of a rationalization). In most cases the destructive impulses, however, are rationalized in such a way that at least few other people or a whole social group share in the rationalization and thus make it appear to be "realistic" to the members of such a group.[29]

It is our fear of dying that makes us powerless and in our desperation we destroy our own shadow by labeling it "evil." This is the mental illness—the human cancer—that out of fear of "the devil" makes us act as if we where God.

Here again our Sufi saint, Rabi´a Al-Adawiyga, comes to our aid by showing us the way out of our madness:

"I love God—I have no time left in which to hate the devil"[30]

Justice and Compassion

Now, of course some people will say that turning the other cheek by focusing on love instead of hate, will make us passive. So, they will ask whether God is a pacifist or not? The trick of logic forces a "yes" to leave the defenseless to die without protection, while a "no" will open the door to more genocide. This is why a new logic that can find the right balance between both yes and no is the best answer.

It is clear that the light of God is unconditional love, but at the same time we live in a physical world that is very much defined by conditional laws. The light is unlimited compassion but at the same time it is also absolute truth that seeks justice. Given that we must live in both dimensions and uphold both laws at the same time, it would only seem practical to find the right balance between opposites.

This is the balance between body and soul, male and female, and in this case the balance between justice and compassion. At the same time, it is the balance between conditional freedom and unconditional freedom, and politically it is the also the balance between Republicans and Democrats, Conservatives and Liberals.

The right balance is needed because in world politics it does seem as if Samuel P. Huntington's prediction in *The Clash of Civilizations?* has gone from theory to fact (at least among those in fear and in power). He predicted that "the clash of civilizations will dominate global politics. The fault lines between civilizations will be the battle lines of the future."[31] He told us that the clash happens through the conflicting pulls of tribalism and globalism.

Polls show that half of the population in America, 49 percent, believes that the tension between Islam and the West is caused by politics. Only 38 percent believe that the clash is due to differences of religion and culture.[32] So, the majority of us see the clash as a political conflict and this fits with the historical development in the region.

As the Roman Empire had expanded its power all the way to Jerusalem, so the Roman Catholic Church also wanted to extend its power through the Crusades. In our time, we see this same struggle going on as Islamic fundamentalism has re-emerged as a response to Western colonialism. Today we should not forget that America (and the Western world) has had its interests in the region for many years. And we must also not be blind of the fact that the U.S. is in no way neutral in the way it interacts with the world. The American empire stretches over 130 countries with more than 700 military bases.[33]

On top of the reaction to American foreign policies, we also live in a world that is changing rapidly where the dynamic of modernism conflicts with its opposite; conservatism. As a person, I sometimes get conservative in my habits, so, I understand that from this position the many ideas of change can seem too radical at times. But at the same time I cannot stop change because change is unstoppable. As we cannot stop the earth from spinning, we cannot stop it from changing.

Change is as true as the seasons and therefore, adaptation through evolution is necessary. However, even in America, not everyone believes in evolution. Polls show that only 28 percent of Americans believe in evolution,[34] and that 55 percent of all Americans (67 % of Bush voters) reject evolution by saying that "God created humans in present form."[35]

I do not wish to get into the debate on evolution vs. creationism, since I believe both are right, but I wanted to point out that there is a lot of objection to change. Conservatism cannot stop the earth from spinning. However, while I do support evolution—change should also take place in a way respectful of the past. Here again the Golden Rule is the key to help us find the right balance between the two extremes of what continues and what disappears—birth and death.

Bauman tells us that the way we change the world today is through "creative destruction"—we build while demolishing at the same time.[36] As we build a new world, we disrespectfully destroy the old. This is how America was built and this is how we are trying to impose Western values on the Middle East today.

There is no love and no respect in this way of evolving. This destruction is chaos within creation and leads to imbalance. Philosopher Jean-Paul Sartre called this creative destruction "life-towards-a-project," where life becomes a path towards a goal. We say that the path and the goal are one, but when we conclude that the goal *is* the path, then life in itself looses value to the higher goal. When the identity and identification of the individual becomes a project—a life project, then this leads away from the true identity of the individual and into a forced social order of mechanical structures. It is these structures that create the identity crisis that leads us into conflict, because the true identity of the individual fights against the imposed constructs.

Life already has a goal in itself—to live—and because life is not just the goal but the path also, there must be freedom to aim at the goal. The goal must not be forced upon humanity with deadly violence. This is not the way to bring up our children or help anyone in this world.

On a personal level, if we do not accept who we are but constantly wish and want to be better, then there is no self-love or self-acceptance. This leads to self-punishment. Most of us know that people who are hard on others are usually harder on themselves. This is a form of immature and unsustainable spiritual development that leads to self-hatred. Self-hatred or the punishment of self and others are not healthy ways to evolve, so one needs to find the right balance. This is no different on a global scale.

In the East some words of wisdom describe this balance: "Do not jab the bull—pull it gently along." A real-life example of these words of wisdom is the difference between Iraq and Turkey. While Iraq has turned out catastrophically, Turkey is evolving in its effort to become a member of the European Union. The end is the same but the means are different.

Bauman lets us know that this lack of acceptance creates a tension between the world *as such* and the world *within reach*.[37] We want the world or ourselves to be different than reality permits, and in this tension we create conflict in our desperation. For the world this means that we punish others for not being like we are or how we want them to be. Cultures and nations are as different as people are and both are at different stages of development. Understanding and respecting this is as important as respecting and understanding ourselves.

The gap between the world as such and the world within reach produces fear and uncertainty. And it is this gap of uncertainty that is dangerous for the world, because as Bauman explains:

> There is a lot of energy boiling in this chaos; with a degree of skill and cunning it can be gathered and redeployed to give the unruliness a direction. The fear...precipitated by powerlessness, is always a tempting weapon to be added to the armory of the power-greedy.[38]

A mature step for our world would be to evolve from creative destruction to respectful creation, from life-towards-a-project to a project-within-life. The equivalent personal step requires us to evolve from letting others make an identity *for* us to claiming our own identity by discovering who we are. By first accepting who we are and where we are, we can with respect and self-love evolve towards our higher self.

In this way, we can have a mindful creation in which we find the right balance between "the goal is the path" and "the path is the goal." This is a sustainable evolution where we evolve on the foundation of the Golden Rule. And then in this sustainable evolution, we can find the right balance between justice and compassion, where as the Light tells us—the goal is not to punish but to teach. By changing perspective from evil to ignorance, we can take out our aggressive intention of wanting to punish and replace it with the enlightened intention of wanting to teach the truth.

Now, what would have been a clash of civilizations can be met with a new logic where the many are not in conflict over either/or, but in cooperation through universal pluralism. This is, however, luckily what the majority of Americans think, since 64 percent believe we can find common ground with the Arab world. Only 31 percent believe that violent conflict is inevitable.[39] (I wonder if these are the same 31 percent that believes in an angry God!?)

Finding common ground is the only reasonable and sustainable response to globalization that can be aligned with the Golden Rule. In this respectful creation we have to take out the tension of evolution by defending life against aggression without becoming that aggression ourselves. This is the right balance between justice and compassion, and evolution into a deeper understanding of the Golden Rule.

The U.S. has been described as a ship with all sails and no anchor. An anchor is a moral foundation and it must be anchored in the Golden Rule. Author Oberby M. Hendricks Jr. explains that, "We must measure every government policy against the yardstick of the commandment to love our neighbor." And if any policy is against the Golden Rule "then that policy is against the politics of Jesus."[40] When we make laws and policies in the physical world, we must not forget to align these with the spiritual law of the Golden Rule.

Standing in the Light, it is very difficult for me to understand how religious America could re-elect and re-establish the horrors created in Iraq. Fortunately this hard-line political wind has changed and I certainly hope that some lessons have been learned. There is still people who want war no matter what, but to make pre-emptive war in the name of God is far from the Light. If we are ignorant, as in the case of the Iraq war, then how can we claim that our actions are just? Being blind we cannot see the right balance between justice and compassion.

Freedom and democracy starts with ourselves, as Jesus says: "First take the plank out of your eye, and then you will see clearly to remove the speck from your brother's eye."[41] And freedom goes as deep as knowing our true identity. This is enlightenment and freedom through the empowerment of the individual.

Erich Fromm explains that, "*The right to express our thoughts, however, means something only if we are able to have thoughts of our own.*"[42] Without knowing who we are, we cannot think for ourselves and thereby we cannot express ourselves freely. If we know who we truly are, then we are free because we have an identity rather than letting others control us.

There are many powers trying to control us, and therefore the right to choose our identity is the key to freedom from these forces. Agreeing with this, Bauman tells us that

> Through focusing on the right to choose one's identity as the sole universality of the citizen/human, on the ultimate, inalienable individual responsibility for the choice—and through laying bare the complex state- or tribe-managed mechanisms aimed at depriving the individual of that freedom of choice and that responsibility.[43]

This individual freedom means that human rights takes center stage and becomes the key to freedom and democracy. The light reflected by the Golden Rule is perfect equality and freedom with the respect for all life. And the life-review is there to teach us the lesson of equality and if we refuse to learn this lesson here on earth, we will learn this lesson ultimately when we meet the light.

In this way, we also see that human rights are based on the Golden Rule. The U.N. Declaration of Human Rights is a good example where the universal principle has been translated into the world of international affairs. Article 1 says, "All human beings are born free and equal in dignity and rights. They are endowed with reason and conscience and should act towards one another in a spirit of brotherhood."[44]

Human rights transcend cultural, religious, and national barriers in the same way that the light transcends these barriers. Founding father of America, Thomas Jefferson said that, "Nothing then is unchangeable but the inherent and inalienable rights of man."[45] The life-review clearly reflects this unchangeable law of the universe that is expressed through the Golden Rule, and so, in our global society this should be the solid foundation on which we build our common future.

Equal human rights are not only reasonable, but they were born out of human darkness in 1948 after the Second World War. The Declaration of Human Rights was not born out of naïve notions, but instead out of the ashes of our darkest moment in human history, as a warning not to repeat the same mistakes again! Life is about learning, not about repeating the same mistake over and over again.

Feed the Source

Darwinism tells us that natural selection works through survival of the fittest, and so the strongest kill the weak as nature works through its levels of the food chain—kill or be killed. However, in the ancient Shamanic traditions, which also incorporate the supernatural world, the same thing is said in a slightly different manner: "Feed the source or the source will feed on you."

This might not sound that different in a world that is strictly materialistic. But if the source of nature is the ultimate reality of the Light, then this ancient way of life gives another meaning. If the source is our true nature and we feed this source through enlightenment, then our survival depends on the essence of our nature which is love. And if the source of life is love—then love is our only survival.

We can also turn this around and say that without love and compassion, we are free to hate our enemy. And when we are able to kill our enemy then what is to stop the enemies we have created from hating and killing us? Love is basic sustainability and the foundation of any family that wishes to prosper and live. It is no different for the human family.

In science, we search for the fundamental level of reality in our quest to know the mind of God. I am confident that the mind of God is not found in outer space but in inner space. It will "require the mind to know itself rather than just to experience itself,"[46] for us to get to know the mind of God. The study of consciousness and meditation is the search for this insight. Through mindfulness and meditation we can directly experience the true nature of the mind, and its nature is the same as the Light.

I believe that the mind of God works on a different principle than Darwinism, whereby we are truly going in the wrong direction by killing each other. Buddhism teaches that it is our mind that makes karma and that this karma controls our physical reality. What we think becomes a force of nature: "All of reality is in the mind, and the mind has us experience it as 'out there.' So we should still take care to see to it that 'out there' is beautiful and not horrible, to prevent the horrible and develop the beautiful."[47]

In this same way it is said that the world is created in the minds of men. Thereby, if our dominant principle of interacting with the world is negative, then we will manifest this negativity and create imbalance in our environment. Here again the human impact on climate change is a present and very clear example of how we interact negatively with our environment out of ignorance. Also war and conflict are very negative ways of interacting with the world that creates instability in our environment.

Erich Fromm tells us that,

> If the process of the development of mankind had been harmonious, if it had followed a certain plan, then both sides of the development—the growing strength and the growing individuation—would have been exactly balanced. As it is, the history of mankind is one of conflict and strife. Each step in the direction of growing individuation threatened people with new insecurities. Primary bonds once severed cannot be mended; once paradise is lost, man cannot return to it.[48]

The mature step in our human evolution is to realize that paradise is not lost—it is here right now—and that we can create more of it through balancing our development. Through respectful creation we can evolve out of our destructive teenage tendencies towards a more harmonious life based on the Golden Rule.

This principle of balance from the Golden Rule can be found everywhere in nature. On a genetic level, the adaptation of a gene to its environment is solely dependent on its preservation or survival.[49] But the principle of balance is also true on a macro level, where the survival of stars and galaxies depend on their ability to achieve harmony. In fact, science tells us that the whole universe is fine-tuned on all levels; the universe is a giant symphony. To survive all levels needs to be in tune and if this applies to the whole universe, it most certainly includes the way we interact with the world.

According to the Anthropic Principle, the whole universe is also described as having purpose on all levels. Every part at every level of the universe has a function by which it performs its purpose. Even a gene at the smallest micro level has a function and this function gives it purpose.

In *The Story of Science,* Robert Augros and George Stanciu tell us that, "A universe aiming at the production of man implies a mind directing it...Though man is not at the physical center of the universe, he appears to be at the center of its purpose."[50] Thereby the whole universe has purpose and our lives in it do have profound meaning.

It would be very logical to conclude that the anthropic principle is what guides the Golden Rule. The Light, as the true nature of reality made of infinite love, would seem to guide this universal symphony. As we are living in a time of great suffering and fear, it would seem very plausible that the Golden Rule is the universal law that will guide us to our survival. Karen Armstrong tells us that the doctrine of compassion is not utopia:

> We must continually remind ourselves that the Axial sages developed their compassionate ethic in horrible and terrifying circumstances... Like us, they were conscious of the void and the abyss. The sages were not utopian dreamers but practical men; many were preoccupied with politics and government. They were convinced that empathy did not just sound edifying, but actually worked. Compassion and concern for everybody was the best policy.[51]

One proof of this was the time of *convivencia* (co-existence) in Spain from around the eight century till the time of the Crusades, which was a period of co-existence between Christians, Jews and Muslims.

In *Constantine's Sword*, James Carroll explains that this period of co-existence is a direct proof that it is possible for us to live together in peace: "That Jews and Christians, together with Muslims, can live in amity, respecting differences while honoring commonalities—that this is no pipe dream—is proven by the fact that, for centuries, they did just that."[52]

This period in time did not last but it existed, and thereby it has left us the living proof that co-existence is possible. In the world today it seems that co-existence is not only a good idea but it could be the only path to our survival. On this path, true dialog to understand each other in a mutual exchange of views can take us into a deeper understanding of the Golden Rule.

It is not enough to impose our ideals on others, even if they might be better; we need to learn to understand the other from within. Then we can begin to help through the right view on reality. This is true compassion and the way through mutual exchange of understanding by which we can reach the Golden Rule.

The United States of America is a great nation and I am speaking as a friend. Its founding fathers are a big part of the creation of this greatness, but the last years have been a fall from grace. Domination through self-interest is not the way to a sustainable future for the world. To be a true world leader, the U.S. needs to re-establish its moral authority and lead in building a world peace upon which we can create the future together with all nations. To be inspired of this kind of greatness, we just need to look back a little.

John F. Kennedy is a testimony of American greatness, and I will let his words inspire true leadership:

> I have, therefore, chosen this time and this place to discuss a topic on which ignorance too often abounds and the truth is too rarely perceived—yet it is the most important topic on earth: world peace. What kind of peace do I mean? What kind of peace do we seek? Not a Pax Americana enforced on the world by American weapons of war. Not the peace of the grave or the security of the slave. I am talking about genuine peace, the kind of peace that makes life on earth worth living, the kind that enables men and nations to grow and to hope and to build a better life for their children—not merely peace for Americans but peace for all men and women—not merely peace in our time but peace for all time.[53]

Fine-Tuning the World

In Judaism we find the Hebrew phrase "Tikkun Olam" which translates into "repairing the world" by setting it in order. This setting in order is the fine-tuning of our world by alignment with the Light and the Golden Rule. I especially like the explanation from the Kabbalist Isaac Luria, who says that God created the world by forming vessels of light to hold the Divine Light. As humans, with a true nature of divine light within us, it then becomes our purpose in life to help God repair the world. Luria explains that,

> If we can raise ourselves to the station where the Divine can see and act through us, then we complete the momentous work of restoring at least one part to the Whole. And so, with the great Kabbalist, we discover a vision of unbounded meaning: perfecting ourselves, perfecting the world, and helping God.[54]

The repairing of the world is the establishment of the Kingdom of God that we know from the Bible. Through the connection of our essence to the Golden Rule, we naturally come to love our neighbor. This means a personal involvement where we are obligated to help others by getting rid of hunger, disease, abuse, oppression, ignorance, and other forms of suffering. The fundamental principle of equality is to wish for others what we wish for ourselves and the Golden Rule demands this equality.

In his book *Ethics for the New Millennium*, the Dalai Lama lets us know that all of our actions have a universal dimension. He says that when we neglect the well-being of others and ignore the universal dimension of our actions, we will end up as seeing our interests separate from the interests of others. Thereby, we are forgetting the fundamental unity of our human family.[55]

This universal perspective with the understanding that others have the same right to happiness as we have helps us to develop a universal responsibility. Science tells us that everything is connected. Through the near-death experience, we can learn that this interconnectedness makes us responsible for our actions.

And because everything is interconnected, Bauman tells us that even freedom is a power relation: "Some people will inevitably be restricted in their choices by the actions I have taken, and they will fail to reach the results *they* wished."[56]

Former President Eisenhower said that weapons take food from the hungry. And when we look at the world budget today, we find that he is absolutely right. We spend more on feeding our fear than we do on feeding our poor, demonstrating that our separation is greater than our interconnection.

In 2004, the total world budget for military expense was 13 times higher than the amount we spent to help the third world countries.[57] As of first quarter 2007, the cost of the war in Iraq was estimated at $ 450 billion adding $ 2 billion a week.[58] Even without thinking of the most needy in our world, this money could have been put to far better use within the U.S.A.

Again it is not the weapons that take the food from the hungry—it is our fear. Fear is the ultimate weapon of control, but in more, it is also our fears that consume the energy of the needy. Fear kills, and by being unaware of this we become the blunt instrument. If America were able to control its fear, there would be fewer reasons to start pre-emptive wars, and both the money and energy spent on war could be put to better use.

Thereby, if we had learned the lessons from Vietnam and Rwanda, then, this energy could have been spent much more wisely. At the beginning of 2007 the body count of the Iraq war was estimated at above 55,000 civilian casualties with over 3,000 American and 5,000 Iraqi military casualties.[59] Even if Iraq does turn for the better years down the line, these lives (and the ones added) are too heavy a price for a change that could come about peacefully with a bit more patience.

At the same time as we have created chaos in Iraq, a silent genocide has been going on in Darfur, Africa, where dictators are not as popular as in the Middle East. Here the estimate of innocent human casualties is estimated at over 200,000 people.[60] Let us say that at least 260,000 people have been killed in the two conflicts. This amounts to *one 9/11 every day* for almost three months!

Actually, I feel bad about counting human life in numbers because life is invaluable. But I wanted to make the point that if we focus our attention on creating stability rather than creating instability, we can implement the Golden Rule with wisdom. Stopping the genocide in Darfur instead of creating chaos in Iraq would have been the better choice, and this proves the point that our interests are not aligned with the Golden Rule quite yet. Here it is funny (tragic) to notice, as some have, that the so-called "pro life" religious right does not care about what happens to life after it enters this world. Where is the true pro life movement of America?

The U.N. is founded on the Golden Rule and has showed itself to have much more wisdom than the U.S. lately. Of course, the U.N. is sometimes unable to act because of the conflicting interests of its members. But here is a chance for the U.S. to show its greatness by supporting the organization to make it stronger rather than making it weaker by splitting it with self-interest.

It is meaningless to talk about democracy in a world that is becoming increasingly smaller if we do not at the same time talk about a global democracy. As tyranny is not sustainable within a country, it is also not sustainable in the world outside. We need the U.N. as our sincere effort to help create a world based on freedom and equality. And even if some people say that the U.N. does not work—well, then, we must make it work. In the same way that we need to build a better democracy in our country, we must also build one for the world.

John F. Kennedy tells us again that,

> To that world assembly of sovereign states, the United Nations, our last best hope in an age where the instruments of war have far out-paced the instruments of peace, we renew our pledge of support: To prevent it from becoming merely a forum for invective; to strengthen its shield of the new and the weak; and to enlarge the area in which its wit may run.[61]

When we have a stable environment in a peaceful world, it is possible for all of us to evolve. We need to build trust through the promise of non-aggression, while protecting the weak with our shield of unity. War and instability is a control mechanism that keeps us all trapped at lower levels of development, so, creating peace is the first step.

When we are at peace, then we can focus all of our attention on helping those in need, which is our obligation. Kennedy also said that, "If a free society cannot help the many who are poor, it cannot save the few who are rich."[62] However, the people of America already know this, and they show their compassion through donations to charity. Not so long ago, I used to only look at the rich as being greedy and stealing the energy of the needy. However, I must admit that 2006 really surprised me in a very positive way.

One of the biggest events of that year to inspire hope was when Warren Buffet donated about $ 37 billion to the Bill and Melinda Gates Foundation. In a world so focused on getting rich, the world's two richest men give their money away to help others. *The Economist* wrote: "It was an extraordinary sight. The world's two richest men hugged each other as a room full of New York's great and good cheered and applauded."[63]

I was truly touched by this great moment and even shed tears of happiness. Since then there has been a lot of talk about the impact of this powerful message. One rumor has it that the super rich, instead of competing to be number one on the Fortune 500, are now competing to be number one on the Slate 60 list of the biggest donors to charity.

At the same time, we also see initiatives of pure intention from powerful and important people from rock stars to ex-presidents. It certainly seems that more and more of us are waking up to the nature of the Light. Even with the war and conflict around us, I am very hopeful. It seems that the many vessels of light are beginning to wake up to their true nature.

His Holiness, the Dalai Lama explains that if we avoid changing our conduct regarding the respect of others and their right to happiness, then soon we will feel the negative consequences. Thus the universal responsibility leads us to a responsibility towards truth.[64] And the truth is closely connected to justice, which demands that we act when we see injustice.

This does not mean that we should respond with anger, but rather react in a constructive way. Thousands of NGO's are working for peace, fair trade, and sustainable development for a better future. At home we can start to implement this level of consciousness by being mindful of where we put our money—what we make grow by feeding our energy— while at the same time being responsible for our footprint in the world. By being mindful of what we take in and what we send out, we can align ourselves in harmony with the Light.

And there is plenty of work to be done. The world teaches us that we are separate and unequal, but the truth is that we are all interconnected and *equal*. This is where evolution is headed—towards the Light—and this direction is the purpose of our lives.

On a personal level you can align yourself with evolution and fit it into your life through many types of personal involvement. The first step is to awaken and get informed about what is going on. Information is power and the more we know the more we can do to change things. Luckily evolution is also freeing the flow of information where the Internet revolution is leading the way.

Here, I really like that *Time* magazine made "YOU" (and me) person of the year 2006. This marks a new stage in our evolution of democracy where the power of information control has been taken back by the people with endless possibilities.

Being informed about the problems we are facing in the world, we can then start to find solutions to these challenges. With freedom of information and the freedom to choose our identity, we can truly live our lives aligned with our true nature. And knowing who we truly are, we will naturally feel that we cannot have knowledge without compassion and thereby we will be motivated to help others.

Since my experience, I have challenged myself to discover the single best thing that I can do to help humanity evolve. How can I do the most good in this life? The answer I came up with was to testify about the Light and help the evolution of human consciousness. At the same time, I also wish to help those who have physical needs. In my near-death experience I felt the pain of all the people suffering in Africa and other poor nations. I truly felt their pain and I still feel their suffering in my heart.

My wife and I sponsor a child (and his community) in Ethiopia, and we also support various organizations with a monthly donation. On top of that, I have also pledged to donate a substantial portion of the proceeds of this book, so that the overflowing profit will benefit the needy rather than making me greedy. You can locate where the profit from this book goes at: www.AwakeningAfterLife.com.

Then I also wish to mention the most positive and needed development in our world, which is the fact that we are finally experiencing that women are being liberated from their oppression. Today we see women as presidents and prime-ministers all over the world. And at the same time, women are becoming the majority at universities and institutes of higher learning in both the Western and

Islamic worlds. These female students of today will be the women leaders of tomorrow.

This is a very positive outlook for the future of humanity. The equality between the sexes means that our world can reach a balance without male overreaction through war and aggression. Also at the same time America faces a very stimulating election in 2008 with the choice between a woman and an Afro-American as the first President of the U.S. Looking back just thirty years in history, this is truly a quantum leap in our evolution and a great outlook for our future development.

Whoever the American people elect as their next President, Democrat or Republican, I hope it will be someone with a balanced mind that can see clearly without blind overreaction. We really need to find a peaceful balance without falling into extremes. Whoever gets to lead must understand the profound responsibility of acting in this world. Plato told us that if someone wanting power truly knew the responsibility that comes with it, no one would want it! Any person with power will have to back down when he or she dies and meets the Light—no one is bigger than God. This is the kind of humility and sense of responsibility that only true greatness can understand.

The world has seen too much war, so what we all need are moderate leaders that will use dialog and diplomacy to reach the goals of its people. And what is our goal? It is to find the right balance between opposites and align our lives in harmony with the cosmos. This is the fine-tuning of existence as we tune in to the universe and begin to create a more beautiful symphony than what has been played before.

The Gospel of Thomas tells us that,

> When you make the two one, and when you make the inside like the outside and the outside like the inside, and then above like the below, and when you make the male and the female one and the same...then will you enter the kingdom.[65]

Chapter Eleven

Final Liberation

When our time is up and we have done what we could here on earth, it is time for us to return to where we came from. This return to source is the return to where we were produced: "When, at the termination of the destruction of the great elements, the final dissolution approaches...Every entity is dissolved into that from which it is produced."[1]

This is the "Supreme Union" where we as a child meet the mother of the universe and become unified with her as our true nature. It is the return to the source of creation itself.

In science this is the Universe at the zero point: zero particles into the mass-less and structure-less state of existence that was before the big bang. This is the entry into another universe and this other realm is the ultimate reality, as a larger space in which our perception of the universe is embedded. Our perception of the universe is a bubble within another bigger space, and when our bubble bursts, we find ourselves in another reality.

What is Heaven?

In the dream that I had after my near-death experience, I returned to the source, totally dissolved into energy. My true nature was energy, and when I finally let go of all my earthly attachments, I returned to this origin of the essence of my being.

This was of course only a dream; however, as I experienced it night after night it seemed not to be merely a dream, but absolutely real to me. After my near-death experience, I had asked myself what would happen if I were to stay in the light and never come back to my body. It is my belief that this is what the dream showed me—my life energy returning to its source.

When I look at science, this understanding seems to make a lot of sense as the particles of my body are dissolved my essence returns to the great sea of energy. Also this fits with a religious understanding of returning to source if we see God as the ground of being.

One near-death account explains my experience of returning home: "It was as if I were going home, so familiar was it to me. As if returning to where I had originally come from...The absolute peace, the oneness, the completeness was the most striking."[2]

When looking at the near-death experience we find that most commonly heaven is described as "the light" rather than a physical place. However, at the same time I am well aware of that many near-death experiences involves meetings with deceased relatives, beings of light or religious figures. So, I have asked myself; why did I not meet a deceased relative, a being of light, or a religious figure?

Researcher Michael Grosso gives one theory where he says that deceased relatives are more likely to appear in experiences that involve literal near-death situations. In cases such as mine, involving a non-literal ego-death situation, he explains that the appearance of deceased relatives would have no purpose.[3]

This could be an explanation and it could also be that as an atheist (before) it would seem understandable that I would not meet a religious figure. I would then opposite expect religious people to meet their religious figures in all cases. However, in this question I find it interesting that for example not all Christians meet God or Jesus.

Don Piper, who was a Christian minister before and after his near-death experience, testifies that he did not actually see God although he knew God was there. He says: "I never saw any kind of image or luminous glow to indicate his divine presence...I saw only a bright iridescence."[4]

Generally, the near-death experience does seem to take the experiencer into the understanding of the God beyond God that Paul Tillich talks about as the ground of being, which underlies our concepts and images. So, the understanding that we can only reach God or heaven through Jesus or someone else, is problematic because the 'real' God seems to be beyond this understanding.

Also Kenneth Ring is in search of the essence of the light or what he calls the "second light." In *Lessons From the Light* he gives us this account from Mellen-Thomas Benedict,

> The Light just reacted and revealed itself on another level, and the message was "Yes, [for] most people, depending on where you

are coming from, it could be Jesus, it could be Buddha, it could be Krishna, whatever." But I said, "But what is it *really?*" And the Light then changed into—the only thing I can tell you [is that] it turned into a matrix.[5]

Benedict calls this matrix our higher self or "the void." He then tells us that, "When I was in the Void, the feeling I had was that I was aware of [things] before I had been created."[6] This matches with my understanding of our true self. And if we remember that the mind or consciousness was earlier explained as a matrix for the light, then this account fits very well with my own experience of the source of the light, as something beyond our images and concepts—as *the light behind God.*

This view is supported by Peter Fenwick, who concludes that,

Although the 'being of light' always has a spiritual significance, it is only seldom that people describe seeing a particular religious figure such as Christ. Even those people whose Christian faith is strong don't always see Christ. Much more often there is a feeling of 'coming before one's maker': the being is felt as 'God' in a very broad sense.[7]

The light is usually the predominate feature at the core of the near-death experience. In his research, Fenwick found that the light was experienced by 72 percent, but he also found that something lay even deeper at the heart of the experience: 88 percent described the experience of the feeling state of calm, peace, or joy. This means that the positive feeling state is the most common feature of the near-death experience.[8]

Fenwick tells us that,

Although many of these visions of Paradise include strong well-formed, visual images, sometimes the imagery is much less pictorial, at times almost losing its form completely. And yet it still remains intensely emotional, and still gives this very strong impression of heightened awareness.[9]

This means that behind whatever visions or images that are experienced, still we find that expanded awareness seems to be the essence of the experience of heaven. It also means that behind whatever being or religious figure we meet, the feelings of peace, joy and love are at the heart of the experience.

My experience was almost without any form at all, and so, I was left with the intense feeling state that Fenwick talks about. Therefore, I also intuitively feel that this feeling state is at the center of the experience and that this could be the essence of the very broad understanding of God and heaven.

Michael Grosso takes this further by explaining that the light is a symbol of consciousness and that the meetings with deceased relatives, out-of-body states, and life-reviews are all manifestations of the light. These manifestations are "extensions of consciousness," as the light is both pure and formless while at the same time it has forms within it.[10]

Grosso compares this explanation to Jung's concept of the self, in that the basic structure of the near-death experience does not seem to be conditioned by the personal, but at the same time there are conditioned variations in the detail of content. This, he says, is equal to Jung's distinction between the archetype as a form without content (non-perceptible), and the archetype as mediated by personal experience (perceptible).[11]

Jung himself told us about the subjective experience that,

> If we approach this task with psychological views that are too personalistic, we fail to do justice to the fact that we are dealing with an archetype which is anything but personal...As archetypes, these figures are semi-collective and impersonal quantities, so that when we identify ourselves with them and fondly imagine that we are most truly ourselves, we are in fact most estranged from ourselves...The personal protagonists in the royal game should constantly bear in mind that at the bottom it represents the "trans-subjective" union of archetypal figures, and it should never be forgotten that it is a *symbolical* relationship whose goal is complete individuation.[12]

Dr. Carlos Alvarado of University of Virginia, who studies out-of-body experiences, has the same view. He tells us that people who have out-of-body experiences where they experience another dimension say that it is a real dimension on a different plane, but at the same time it interacts with the mentality of the individual.[13]

This interaction with our mind becomes the symbolical relationship with the light, which means that we create the content of the experience within the light. Researcher Jeffrey Long calls the experience a "co-created experience" of both personal and impersonal events.[14]

In addition to this, P. M. H. Atwater also claims that the "other worlds" that are encountered in the near-death experience do not seem to have their own independent existence. She explains that the light seems to be non-physical; rather than the light originating from other worlds, it seems more like these other worlds have their origin from within the light.[15]

Melvin Morse agrees with this perspective, saying that emotional archetypes are incorporated into the experience by the beholder in order to help make sense of the experience.[16] Also if the meetings or other worlds did have their own independent existence, it would seem odd that some studies find that the meetings are not only with relatives who are deceased but also with people who are still alive.[17]

Having said this, I wish to emphasize that the near-death experience is a subjective experience that is co-created with the personality of each person. We are all unique individuals. It is not my intention to change anyone's idea of heaven or take anything away from anybody. We are all entitled to our beliefs and I fully accept people who choose Jesus or someone else as their guide into heaven.

It is only when people hold on to their choice of belief so hard that they become fundamentalists that I see a problem. Here I am talking about people who believe and preach that Jesus is the only way by saying that those who die without Christ will go to hell. This is a problem that we see expressed throughout the world through war and conflict. To avoid this, I prefer to see heaven and its gate from a more universal perspective. This is also why I choose to align my experience with a more open interpretation that has room for other people's beliefs.

Fenwick says about the broad understanding of God that, "Perhaps 'neutrally spiritual' is the nearest one can get to the feeling the being evokes."[18] I did not meet a being or figure, except one could say that the light itself was the nature of being, and therefore, I also prefer the term *neutrally spiritual*. For me, this term describes my experience correctly as the nature of the light being a neutral spiritual energy from a God beyond God.

Quantum physics uses the term *duality* to evoke the understanding that one and the same phenomenon can be viewed from different perspectives. So the experience of the near-death phenomenon can be *both* personal *and* impersonal, while still being the experience of the same ultimate reality.

At the ultimate level, everything is one because everything is interconnected. This is what Pim van Lommel explained earlier; at the fundamental level of the universe there is no objectivity, only subjective experience. From this he concludes that there are no real objective results whereby we will have to change our concepts of objectivity.[19]

Buddhism teaches the same, that relative and absolute truth are two sides of the same truth and thereby one and the same. In the same way, meeting relatives or religious figures and not meeting anyone are also two sides of the same truth. This type of logic represents the way out of fundamentalism where the two extremes fight each other.

Ultimately the exact nature of the near-death experience is unknown. This indescribable phenomenon is related to us through subjective means and we are thus in the dark about its full mystery. Bruce Greyson reminds us that the near-death experience is like the Indian story of the five blind men trying to describe an elephant. We are the blind people trying to understand and describe the ultimate nature of the universe, and while being unable to see we hold on to pieces of the absolute truth thinking that's how the whole elephant—the whole truth—must be.

Meeting the Light

Even though we cannot determine (or agree on) exactly what heaven will look like, and who or what will be there waiting for us, I still believe that it is possible to provide some psychological insight on how to get there. Since the feeling state with its heightened awareness seems to be at the heart of the experience of the Light, or heaven, I am able to guide towards it based on my personal experience. Having touched the elephant, I am able to describe what my part of it felt like, and thereby I am able to share at least one part of it. I believe that the deepest elements of my experience are what Kenneth Ring calls "the ultimate lessons of the light."

Ring tells us that,

> Those who are blessed enough to travel there are the persons who are perhaps best equipped to express for us what might fairly be called "the ultimate lessons of the Light," from which, using a phrase associated with the world's great spiritual traditions, the essential "wisdom teachings" of the NDE can be extracted.[20]

For some reason, of all the wisdom teachings of the spiritual traditions, the one that describes my experience the best is *The Tibetan Book of the Dead*. And at the essence of my experience is what is at heart of Buddhism and most other traditions: The true self.

Dying is the hardest event to handle in our lives, and therefore, the crossover into the light can be an extreme event. Raymond Moody tells us that, "Many people find the notion of being out of their bodies so unthinkable that, even as they are experiencing it, they feel conceptually quite confused about the whole thing and do not link it with death for a considerable time."[21]

The next dimension is truly beyond anything we can imagine, therefore the confusion. This was certainly my experience. The intense power of leaving my body was so strong that I perceived it as a powerful explosion. Earlier I explained that the only thing in this world that comes close to describing the feeling is the pull of gravity in free fall.

I know a Buddhist center where the Lama takes his students sky diving in order to practice mindfulness during the free fall. I have personally practiced my mindfulness while putting up banners for Greenpeace on high buildings and structures. These levels above the ground would normally make me black out from the fear of heights (which I really had in the beginning), but I learned to focus my mind and hold on to my mindfulness.

Even though I have tested the strength of my mindfulness in this way, I do not think this extreme measure is necessary. However, I do believe that it is a good idea to train our mindfulness in some form, because as Michael Grosso suggests; the less we are prepared for merging with the light, the more we will recoil from this meeting.[22]

This is certainly something that I can confirm from my experience, because the dimension of the light can simply be too powerful for a mind that is unprepared. Therefore, preparing ourselves to meet this light will help us merge with it and enter the door to heaven.

In the Tibetan Book of the Dead, we are told that when the relative mind, or subjective mind that has clouded the enlightened mind, has fallen away, then we will meet the ultimate reality in the form of the clear light. This is the dissolution of the gross awareness of the senses that are connected to the elements, "where consciousness itself dissolves into the all-encompassing space of truth."[23]

The clear light nature is free of all points of subjectivity, and therefore difficult for the subjective awareness to enter into. Our habit of being present on a subjective level becomes solid if this is all that we know. Thereby, the heavy momentum of our subjective awareness creates a fear of losing this sense and a fear of letting go.[24]

If all we know is the subjective awareness, then giving this perspective up, can seem like giving up life. So by instinct we will fight to keep this subjective perspective, as we would fight to stay alive. This is what we call the death struggle on this side of life, and this lack of acceptance of the ultimate reality can cause problems in our merger with the light.

What makes death painful is that when we come from an unenlightened state of awareness, we are passing over into a different and unknown state of awareness. And with the fear of the unknown, this makes death a painful experience, because we hold on to the state of awareness from which we've come. Thereby it is the fear that makes death painful. It is the fear of letting go of the habit of being present in a subjective state of awareness.

Sogyal Rinpoche explains that,

> If we have had instructions on the meaning of death, we will know what enormous hope there is when the Ground Luminosity (or Clear Light) dawns at the moment of death. However, there still remains the uncertainty of whether we will recognize it or not, and this is why it is so important to stabilize the recognition of the nature of mind through practice while we are still alive.[25]

The Dividing Line

The Bhagavadagita describes that there are two ways of leaving this world—one is in light and the other is in darkness. If we pass from this dimension in light we will not come back, but if we pass in darkness we will return.[26] The near-death experience gives testimony of people passing in both ways, and we find evidence of a clear border or point of no return. Therefore, also near-death researchers claim that the entry into Paradise is not automatic.[27]

Jung told us how we can lose ourselves in this passing over to the other side by either a positive or negative inflation of the ego:

> If the individual identifies himself with the contents awaiting integration, a positive or negative inflation results. Positive inflation comes very near to a more or less conscious megalomania; negative inflation is felt as an annihilation of the ego.[28]

The content is what Margot Grey refers to as "unfinished business," and she explains that it is this attachment that becomes trapped in the psyche, or soul, which then continues to cause problems until recognized and overcome. There is an emotional charge behind this content which creates the attachment, and thereby our energy is blocked along with our progress.[29]

She further explains that the way to free ourselves from this blockage is by realizing that, "heaven and hell are not places to which we 'go' when our earthly life is ended, but rather a 'state' which we create ourselves and which can be changed by us at any moment."[30]

Freeing our energy from blockage is what Jung calls the "supreme aim." To make oneself conscious of the contents that have been projected within our mind—conscious realization—is the supreme aim.[31] And therefore the dividing line between the light and the darkness becomes the key to passing from this world into the next.

The Tibetan Book of the Dead calls this the "border line between going up and going down," and reveals that at this border it is "the time when by concentrating for an instant you will enjoy constant happiness."[32] In the Buddhist tradition the key to concentrating the mind is to focus on non-attachment, or emptiness, which is reached through a mind in equilibrium. This state is our true nature and the absolute nature of reality. This is who we truly are, and by concentrating on our true identity—remembering who we are—the door to eternal happiness is open to us.

Buddhism uses meditation to train this state of mind as we discussed in chapter six. Dream Yoga is also practiced to heighten awareness by cultivating mindfulness in the dream state as a practice of awareness in dying. According to Buddhism, dreams come from the same karmic patterns that control our mind when we are awake. And therefore the dream state is used as a practice for entering the state of dying when we leave the body.

Many of us are familiar with lucid dreaming, which is the awakening within a dream. I have had many lucid dreams, and I believe that practicing mindfulness in dreams is a good way of training awareness of dying. But in crossing the dividing line from this dimension to the next, I am also convinced that the power of love can take us very far.

When I was going through my negative life-review in my near-death experience, it was clearly when I connected to love that I was liberated from this negative state. As I went through all the pain that I had caused others and all the pain and suffering of the world we live in, it was the change to a loving and compassionate state of mind that got me out of it.

Another experiencer, Howard Storm explains the same in the movie *The Search for Heaven*:

In my desperation I yelled out into the darkness: Jesus, please help me. With that a tiny light appeared in the darkness and became very bright. It was the most brilliant and beautiful light that lifted me up and filled me with ecstasy. And I knew absolutely that this was the Jesus that I knew as a child. He took me out of that horrible place that I now know is hell. And we began to approach heaven…The most profound moment in my near-death experience was when Jesus came to me in that darkness, and all my hopelessness, and unbelief, and disappear, and self-pity was replaced by love and acceptance and joy.[33]

Near-death researcher, Nancy Evans Bush, who has been investigating negative experiences for more than two decades, agrees with this. Her conclusion is that either to "surrender" or "call for help" is what liberates a person from the negative experience and opens the door to the light.[34]

This makes sense from a Buddhist perspective because non-attachment does not mean that the true nature of reality is actually empty—it is filled with love and compassion. The ultimate reality is "emptiness with a core of compassion," and so enlightenment can be reached even without vast learning. If we either remember our true nature or think of its quality as love and compassion, we will end up in the same place—in "the unity of emptiness and compassion."[35]

The Buddhist guide to liberation reveals that, "Because the essence of these disturbing emotions is wisdom, it is possible to be liberated by recognizing their nature."[36] This is also where the teacher or master comes in as a helping guide towards enlightenment. The devotion towards a teacher has a profound purpose because of "the connection between the blessings of the master's enlightened mind, your own openness of faith and the truth of dharmata which is the natural state of wakefulness."[37]

In short, the faith and devotion towards a teacher connects us to the enlightened energy of the true nature of reality. What this means is that if we have developed a habit or reflex of praying during difficult times in our lives, these prayers can now lead us into the light when we die. By remembering our teacher, or any great holy person like for example Christ, with all our heart and devotion, we will connect to the enlightened energy of love and compassion by the power of their blessing.

The true nature of reality is behind many different paths, and whatever tool we use to get there is not important. All we have to remember is that its essence is love and compassion. It loves us as a mother loves a child and we become unified in the Supreme Union by remembering the love that shines from the essence of this source.

We can learn the same from the Sufi tradition. Here Rabi'a Adawiya tells us about a secret that will scare hell away: "O Lord, if you send me to hell on the morrow of the resurrection, I will reveal a secret such that hell will flee from me, not to return for a thousand years."[38]

This is also what we find in the Bible. In Psalm 138 we are told that God is always present: "If I ascend into heaven, thou will be there. If I lay down in Hell, thou are there!"

The true nature of reality is love, and thereby God's love is always there with us even behind our own creation of hell. So, to get out of hell, all we have to do is remember this and think of love. This is also what we learn from the near-death experience where the love and compassion of the light is always present behind whatever we might project in it. The homecoming of feeling absolute love, peace, and joy is the essence of the light that lies at the heart of the experience. This is the secret that will make hell flee from us.

Also Dante told us about entering the gates of heaven: "the only way to pass is through the heart center." In *The Dreamers Book of the Dead*, Robert Moss explains that, "If you are not yet ready to trust yourself to the saving power of love, you are not prepared for death—or for life."[39] This is ultimately true and at the same time the reason, that love is the only win/win situation. By choosing love while we live in this world, we win in both this dimension and the next.

Recognizing the Light

In the Buddhist understanding of enlightenment, it is not enough to see or meet the light—we need to become one with it. This merger happens through the ability of being able to recognize the clear light, and therefore this is why we find a lot of emphasis on this in *The Tibetan Book of the Dead*.

In my case, I clearly experienced being part of the light, realizing it was my true nature. It was as if after leaving my body, I become one with the light. This was the experience of truth—the true nature of reality, and I experienced this as the ultimate homecoming.

This is generally described in the near-death experience as being "enveloped in light and love," and with having no sense of separate identity. One person testifies that, "I was the light and one with it."[40] While some people see the light as a barrier and a point of no return, it is clear that other people directly describe entering the light.[41]

I experienced this as being pure mind of unbound awareness. This is what Raymond Moody calls people feeling as if they are "pure consciousness," where they are able to see everything around them.[42] Also in the research of Kenneth Ring, we found the "transcendental awareness" (mindsight) where people were able to see everything in a 360 degree angle around them.[43]

The Bardo Guidebook to the Tibetan Book of the Dead teaches that our mind within the physical body is like the space within a jar. At the moment when we die and leave the body, "the jar breaks, the space within and without merge...consciousness merges with the primordially pure nature, the ground luminosity."[44]

The ground luminosity is the true nature of reality expressed through the clear light. In the Tibetan Book of the Dead the true nature of the mind is the true nature of reality. This absolute nature of our mind is empty and this emptiness is in fact the light: "Inseparable from emptiness is the luminosity—the presence of what is real."[45]

Now, here I must be humble and admit that the Tibetan Book of the Dead is much more complicated than my experience and the individual stories of near-death experiences. This text describes different *bardos*, or intermediate states, and many places that are sometimes featured in near-death experiences have a different meaning in the Tibetan tradition. For example, entering a beautiful city would mean that one would be reborn as a human, and entering a white light means that one would be born as a God.[46] A full understanding of this traditional text requires intensive studies or teachings from a master.

Still, one thing is clear. We all have the same experience when we die, and enlightenment in both life and death comes from the knowledge of our true nature—who we truly are. And so, the Tibetan Book of the Dead reveals a great deal about the moment of enlightenment at death, and reminds us, "At this moment, know thou thyself; and abide in that state."[47]

The true nature of the mind is like a cloudless sky where "the naked spotless intellect is like unto a transparent vacuum without circumference or center."[48] This was very much like my experience, and one of the most important masters in the Tibetan tradition, Milarepa, told us that, "The Dharma-Kaya of thine own mind thou shalt see; and seeing That, thou shalt have seen the All—The Vision Infinite, the Round of Death and Birth and the State of Freedom."

Near-death researcher, Peter Fenwick says that often people have a feeling of profound knowledge, and a realization that they have been given the answer to all the secrets in the universe. One account describes that "I understood I was born on earth and knew the answer to every mystery," and another account; "Enlightenment is the wonder, and here I understood the universe."[49]

Raymond Moody also found that people got brief glimpses into a separate realm of existence in which "all knowledge—whether of past, present, or future—seemed co-exist in sort of timeless state," and this was experienced as a moment of enlightenment with complete knowledge.[50]

The Tibetan Book of the Dead teaches us that to reach enlightenment by recognizing the light of our mind it must be free from darkness or obscuration. The clear light is "a state of minimum distraction," which means that the mind must be calm and undisturbed: "The natural state is totally free from any mental constructs, whether good or bad...it is perfectly empty."[51]

Therefore, from a Buddhist perspective our consciousness should be free of either a positive or negative influence from the life-review. Both my life-review and preview took me out of the light, so my experience fits with the understanding that the mind needs to be clear and empty without images or projections.

The state of the mind in which to recognize the light is described as "self-contained in its own nature like water poured into water, just as it is, loose, open and relaxed."[52] In this state, by knowing our true nature, we can hold on to the light: "When the light arises, hold that thought" because "one is instantly liberated by the mere understanding of the identification."[53]

Here there is a distinction between white light and clear light, where the normal white light we know from this dimension is not the same as the clear light of the mind. For me, it was a kind of transparent light, which fits with the Buddhist description of clear light:

> The subtlest light that illuminates the profoundest reality of the universe...It is an inconceivable light, beyond the duality of bright and dark, a light of self-luminosity of all things. Hence "transparency" is a good rendering, as is "clear light," as long as "clear" is understood as "transparent" and not as "bright."[54]

We can also find similar descriptions of the light in the near-death experience, where people do not only use the color white to describe it.

Generally it is a very bright light (without hurting the eyes) that is very difficult to describe as being "unearthly" or having an "indescribable brilliance."[55]

The Buddhist tradition tells us about this "mind light" that, "Whoever can *hold* this light will experience the limitless awareness and highest bliss of enlightenment. All separation between space and energy, here and there, past, present, and future then falls away."[56]

At this point we will experience the fundamental truth of reality where all dualities merge into transcendent oneness and we experience the Supreme Joy.[57] This is exactly what we find in the near-death experience when people relate the joy and ecstasy of experiencing the light. We also have the experience of absolute peace and oneness, and it is this feeling of completeness that defines the sense of "coming home." This is described, as Fenwick told us, "as if they had always known this state and that birth, life with its pains, and death, are all departures from an underlying consciousness."[58]

Fenwick adds that it seems probable that this emotional state is primary and spreads into the images that arise in the near-death experience. Because nearly 90 percent of the accounts in his study described feelings of peace or joy during their experience, he concludes that this heightened awareness with the "feeling state" is the essence of the near-death experience.[59] And as we saw earlier, the feeling state is then at the heart of the experience—what we call heaven.

This feeling state is an immensely powerful sensation, and Soygal Rinpoche lets us know about the clear light that, "Even though the Ground Luminosity presents itself naturally to us all, most of us are totally unprepared for its sheer immensity, the vast and subtle depth of its naked simplicity."[60] For me, it was an incredibly powerful sensation to meet the light, which I have described as an internal explosion of gravity pulling my atoms apart.

In Dante's Gate of Fire we find that, "There, where the ascending light from your heart meets heaven's fire, you will encounter your radiant guide, the soul of your soul. There, in that place of luminous encounter, you will become one."[61] Dante calls it the meeting with "heaven's fire" and this is the sheer immensity of merging with the light.

So, how do we prepare for a meeting of such overwhelming power? The guide through heaven's fire in my experience, and in Buddhism, is the mind as the soul of the soul. The essence of the experience is the mind, and therefore, knowing who we are becomes the rock in this wild river. Buddhism teaches that people who do not reach enlightenment do so either because they do not recognize the clear light or because they are not able to remain in its continuity.[62]

To train in the continuity of the ultimate nature of the clear light means to practice a state of wakefulness—resting in who we are, whether we meditate on emptiness or practice mindfulness while doing other activities in our everyday lives. "Luminosity refers to what is actual; simply that which is naturally present...training in it means simply maintaining a continuity of wakefulness."[63]

Wakefulness is simply the true nature of the mind free from mental constructs. The true nature of reality is the nature of things as they are. The space outside the mind is empty and unconditioned, and enlightenment is simply the realization that the mind is in essence that space of naked awareness. Through this realization the space inside can merge with the space outside like a river flowing naturally into the sea and liberation is instant.

The Ultimate Reality

"Most believe at the moment of death the person dies and the Universe goes on, but could it be that *the Universe dies* and the person goes on?"[64]

Yes, this is very much my experience—my universe died as I awoke to the true nature of reality. This was my awakening after life. Even though I did not die, I left my body and this world to experience the ultimate reality, and this has given me the ability to share this story. My single motivation for writing this book has been to testify to this absolute reality—*the Truth* beyond what we can see with our eyes. It does exist, even though some of us do not see it because we have been cut off from its source. However, sooner or later we will all have to experience it because we are all *in* it.

The Tibetan Book of the Dead describes this state as "the eternally blissful union of bliss awareness," and reveals that it is the "ultimate reality as the ultimate lover, experiencing voidness as a total mental and physical union between oneself as orgasmic bliss."[65]

This eternal orgasmic bliss of absolute love is what is on the other side of the door to eternal life. This is what awaits us in the next dimension. This is the ultimate reality of life, in a dimension that is far beyond anything we can imagine in this world. And it is love—it is *all* love—beyond our wildest imagination.

Now, of course one could ask what happens to me—"I"—in this explosion of love? His Holiness, the Dalai Lama explains that, "there is only the very subtle energy-mind, and upon that basis you can impute the very subtle person or 'I.' At that time there isn't any gross 'I' at all, so the two—the gross self and the very subtle self—do not manifest simultaneously."[66]

Jung also explains this:

> The union of the conscious mind or ego-personality with the unconscious personified as anima produces a new personality compounded of both...Not that the new personality is a third thing midway between conscious and unconscious, it is both together. Since it transcends consciousness it can no longer be called "ego" but must be given the name of "self"...The self too is both ego and non-ego, subjective and objective, individual and collective. It is the "uniting symbol" which epitomizes the total union of opposites.[67]

For me, it was clearly this experience of the self. After my experience of ego-death I left my body and entered the ultimate reality in a powerful sensation as if I was dissolved in a massive explosion of pure love. Outside my body I became one with infinite space of unbound awareness. My consciousness had no boundaries and I had all the knowledge in the whole universe.

This was my true nature of eternal and unlimited love beyond human comprehension. My essence was one with the universe; I was it and it was me. This was the true nature of reality as the fundamental truth of everything. All is one—everything is connected—and it is ALL Love.

So, where was "I"—my ego? It had died in this profound revelation and what was left was a new me united with everything; individual and collective, in total oneness. The reality that I believed in before was dead, and what was born in its place was a new understanding of the ultimate truth of reality. To be reborn in this new reality, all we have to do is surrender to it—surrender to the love—by remembering *it is* love.

In *The Dreamers Book of the Dead*, Robert Moss shares this beautiful account by Mary:

> This gate is invisible...I am merged with Jesus and merged with the light and merged with the vast wings of the eagle and one with

God. Wave upon wave of energy sweeps through "me." I say "me" in quotes because I have ceased to exist as the person I am in the phenomenal world, and instead am simply energy, light, and joy. "My" consciousness is connected to this vastness, this love, this energy. I am but I am not. I am everything, nothing...Am I afraid of losing myself? No, because in this light, I still am so much more. I am not in this heavy body. I am a part of the singing light. As soon as I relax, I am back in the light again.[68]

The energy of love is the spirit in pure form. By identifying with this pure energy, our true self, we become one with the flow of energy in the universe. All we have to do is to hold on to who we are and surrender to God—the ultimate reality—as pure and unbound love. In this flow of love, we are truly alive and in eternal existence.

This is the awakening to eternal life. This is the final frontier of our evolution, and the gateway to the endless universe. It is a cosmic journey in orgasmic bliss into the eternal existence. It is the entry into another dimension of absolute and infinite love beyond our comprehension.

Therefore, for lack of words, I will let the testimonies from other near-death experiencers speak for themselves:

If that is dying, it's nothing to be afraid of. It's wonderful.[69]

It was in all forms of communication, sights, sounds, thoughts. It was any- and everything. It was as if there was nothing that wasn't known. All knowledge was there, not just in one field, but everything.[70]

It seemed that all of a sudden, all knowledge—of all that had started from the very beginning, that would go on without end—that for a second I knew all the secrets of all ages, all the meaning of the universe, the stars, the moon—of everything.[71]

A peace that I can only describe as heavenly.[72]

There was a tremendous sense of peace, love, compassion and understanding.[73]

It was warm; it was radiant; it was peaceful; it was accepting; it was forgiving; it was completely non-judgemental; and it gave me a sense

of total security the likes of which I had never known. I loved it. It
was perfection; it was total, unconditional love. It was anything and
everything you would wish for on earth.[74]

The only way I can describe it, is pure bliss and love.[75]

It was overwhelmingly evident that the Light loved everyone equally
without *any* conditions. I really want to stress this because it made
me so happy to know we didn't have to believe or do certain things
to be loved. WE ALREADY WERE AND ARE, NO MATTER
WHAT.[76]

I really not only felt immortal, I felt as if I had existed forever, my
being and 'soul' had been this way before.[77]

It was as if I were going home, so familiar was it to me. As if
returning to where I had originally come from...The absolute
peace, the oneness, the completeness, was the most striking...Now
I understood something more about God being the Omega and
Alpha of the whole existence...[the experience] has left me with a
striking awareness of our very transitory existence here, through life
itself; also that that other afterworld is far more real than this one
ever is.[78]

[The questions] concerned existence, the meaning and purpose of
life and the universe itself. I could not possibly know the answers
but I did![79]

I KNEW completely without any shadow of a doubt that it was
the strongest force in existence. It was the Energy of Pure Love. I
thought, "I can't wait to tell people."[80]

I wanted to sob with pure joy at the perfection of all creation.[81]

The light was extremely concerned and loving towards all people. I
can remember looking at the people together and the light asking

me to love the people. I wanted to cry, I felt so deeply for them...I thought, "If they could only know how much they're loved, maybe they wouldn't feel so scared or lonely anymore."[82]

Endnotes

Chapter One

[1] Soygal Rinpoche, *The Tibetan Book of Living and Dying*, 11.

Chapter Two

[1] IANDS, www.iands.org/about NDEs.
[2] Atwater, *The Complete Idiot's Guide to Near-Death Experiences*, 39.
[3] Long, *Near-Death Experience*, www.nder.org, Overview.
[4] Atwater, *The Complete Idiot's Guide to Near-Death Experiences*, 141.
[5] Morse, *Transformed by the Light*, 194.
[6] Grof, *Psychology of the Future*, 294.
[7] Noyes; Greyson, Flynn, *The Near-Death Experience*, 272.
[8] Greyson, E-mail reply after taking NDE test, November 9, 2006.
[9] Atwater, *The Complete Idiot's Guide to Near-Death Experiences*, 8.
[10] Woodruff on Larry King Live, CNN, March 1, 2007.
[11] Van Lommel, *Near-Death experiences in survivors of cardiac arrest*, The Lancet, Vol. 358, December 15, 2001.
[12] Interview in *The Day I Died: The Mind, the Brain, and Near-Death Experiences*, British Broadcasting Corporation, 2002 / Films for the Humanities & Sciences, 2005.
[13] Holden, *Veridical Perception in Near-Death Experiences*, IANDS Conference, October 27, 2006.
[14] IANDS, www.iands.org.
[15] Grey, *Return From Death*, 23.
[16] Piper, *90 Minutes in Heaven*, 201-202.
[17] Atwater, *The Complete Idiot's Guide to Near-Death Experiences*, 184.
[18] Atwater, *The Complete Idiot's Guide to Near-Death Experiences*, 211.
[19] Fenwick and Fenwick, *The Truth in the Light*, 134.
[20] Grey, *Return From Death*, 85.
[21] Ring, Valarino, *Lessons from the Light*, 81.

22   Ring, Valarino, *Lessons from the Light,* 75.

23   Ibid, 81.

24   Ibid, 78.

25   Ibid, 80.

26   Atwater, *The Complete Idiot's Guide to Near-Death Experiences,* 172.

27   Ring, Valarino, *Lessons from the Light,* 95.

28   Van Lommel, *Near-Death experiences in survivors of cardiac arrest,* The Lancet, Vol. 358, December 15, 2001, page 2044.

29   IANDS, www.iands.org.

30   IANDS, www.iands.org.

31   Ibid.

32   Ring, *Heading Towards Omega,* 53.

33   Grey, *Return From Death,* 107.

34   Ring, *Heading Toward Omega,* 316.

35   Ring, *Heading Toward Omega,* 156.

36   Lewis, *The Death and Afterlife Book,* xiii.

37   Grey, *Return From Death,* 188.

38   CBS News, New York, Oct. 30, 2005.

39   Phipps, Interview with Bruce Greyson, 05.09.16, www.wie.org/reincarnation.

40   Atwater, *The Complete Idiot's Guide to Near-Death Experiences,* 276.

41   Moody, *Life After Life,* 34.

42   Moody, *Life After Life,* 50.

43   Ibid, 42, 43.

44   Ibid, 63.

45   Ibid, 59.

46   Fenwick, Fenwick, *The Truth in the Light,* 10.

47   Fenwick, Fenwick, *The Truth in the Light,* 58.

48   Moody, *Life After Life,* 96.

49   Moody, *Life After Life,* 97.

50   Grey, *Return from Death,* 48.

51   Moody, *Life After Life,* 47.

52   Moody, *Life After Life,* 66.

53   Ibid, 64, 65.

Chapter Three

1   Abernethy, *Exploring Religious America,* Religion & Ethics Newsweekly, April 26, 2002.

2   Merriam-Webster's Collegiate Dictionary, 10th Edition, 985.

3   Atwater, *The Complete Idiot's Guide to Near-Death Experiences*, 291.

4   Fenwick, Fenwick, *The Truth in the Light*, 1.

5   Fenwick, Fenwick, *The Truth in the Light*, 22-23.

6   Grey, *Return From Death*, 186.

7   Fenwick, Fenwick, *The Truth in the Light*, 23.

8   *Exploring Religious America*, Religion & Ethics Newsweekly, April 26, 2002.

9   Wong, *Scientific American*, Vol. 16, 2, 2006, 76.

10   Budge, *The Egyptian Book of the Dead; The Doctrine of Eternal Life*, lxx - lxxi

11   Budge, *The Egyptian Book of the Dead*; The Doctrine of Eternal Life, lxxi-lxxii.

12   Ibid, lxiv.

13   Ibid, lxx.

14   Telang, *The Bhagavadagita*, Chapter XIII, 103.

15   Telang, *The Bhagavadagita*, Chapter XIII, 103.

16   Ibid, Chapter X, 89.

17   Ibid, Chapter XIII, 105.

18   Ibid, Chapter XIV, 109.

19   Telang, *The Bhagavadagita*; Anugita, Chapter XXVII, 335.

20   Ibid.

21   Ibid.

22   Thurman, *The Tibetan Book of the Dead*, 121.

23   Ibid, 119-120.

24   Ibid, 122.

25   Ponlop, *The Two Truths*, Shambhala Sun, May 2006, 45.

26   Yates, *Jung on Death and Immortality*, 133.

27   Holy Bible, *New Testament*, 1 Corinthians 15:13+14.

28   Holy Bible, NT, 1 Corinthians 15:15+18.

29   Robinson, The Testimony of Truth; *The Nag Hammadi Library*, 451.

30   Ibid, 454.

31   Ibid, 455.

32   Ibid, 455.

33   Holy Bible, *New Testament*, John 3:14.

34   Pagels, *The Gnostic Gospels*, 31.

35   Pagels, *The Gnostic Gospels*, 39.

36   Carroll, *Constantine's Sword*, 284.

37   Holy Bible, *NT*, 1 Corinthians 15:50.

38   Ibid, John 3:5

39   Ibid, John 3:8

40   Ibid, 1 Corinthians 15:40.
41   Ibid, 1 Corinthians 15:42-44.
42   Robinson, The Dialogue of the Savior, *The Nag Hammadi Library*, 251.
43   Pagels, *The Gnostic Gospels*, 111.
44   Pagels, *The Gnostic Gospels*, xx.
45   Carroll, *Constantine's Sword*, 284,
46   The Holy Bible, *New Catholic Version*, Old Testament., Genesis, 1:3-4.
47   Holy Bible, *New Testament*, John, 1:4.
48   Holy Bible, *NT,* John, 1:9.
49   Ibid, 1 John 1:5.
50   Ibid, 1 John 4:16.
51   Robinson, The Gospel of Thomas, 50, *The Nag Hammadi Library*, 132.
52   Robinson, The Gospel of Thomas, 24, *The Nag Hammadi Library*, 129.
53   Holy Bible, NT, John, 1:10-11.
54   Holy Bible, NT, John, 1:12.
55   Pagels, *Beyond Belief*, 67.
56   Pagels, *Beyond Belief*, 68.
57   Robinson, The Gospel of Thomas, 3; *The Nag Hammadi Library*, 126.
58   Pagels, *Beyond Belief*, 68.
59   Robinson, The Gospel of Thomas, 3; *The Nag Hammadi Library*, 126.
60   Ring, *Heading Towards Omega*, 152.
61   Ring, *Heading Towards Omega*, 151.
62   Telang, *The Bhagavadagita*, Chapter X, 89.
63   Telang, *The Bhagavadagita*; The Anugita, Chapter XXVII, 335.
64   Holy Bible, Ephesians 4:6.
65   The Holy Bible, *New Catholic Version*, Exodus, 3:14.
66   The Holy Bible, *New Catholic Version*, Exodus, 3:14, footnote.
67   Robinson, The Sophia of Jesus; *The Nag Hammadi Library*, 222.
68   Ibid, 223.
69   Ibid, 227.
70   Ibid, 225.
71   Ibid, 230.
72   Pagels, *The Gnostic Gospels*, 32.
73   Pagels, *The Gnostic Gospels*, 33.
74   Ibid, 37.
75   Telang, *The Bhagavadagita*, Chapter X, 88.
76   Pagels, *The Gnostic Gospels*, xix-xx.

Chapter Four

1   Armstrong, *The Great Transformation*, 326.
2   Kant, *Prolegomena*, § 48, 102.
3   The Barna Group, *Americans Are Most Likely to Base Truth on Feelings*, February 12, 2002, www.barna.org.
4   The Barna Group, *Americans Are Most Likely to Base Truth on Feelings*, February 12, 2002, www.barna.org.
5   Ibid.
6   Giberson, *The Man Who Fell to Earth*, Science & Spirit, www.science-spirit.org.
7   Desmond, *Being and the Between*, 463.
8   Desmond, *Being and the Between*, 463.
9   Atwater, *The Complete Idiot's Guide to Near-Death Experiences*, 291.
10   Armstrong, *The Great Transformation*, 316.
11   Jowett, *Plato: The Republic*, Book VI, 174.
12   Churton, *Gnostic Philosophy*, 369.
13   Fenwick, Fenwick, *The Truth in the Light*, 73.
14   Fenwick, Fenwick, *The Truth in the Light*, 135.
15   Piper, Murphey, *90 Minutes in Heaven*, 201-202.
16   Hick, *The Fifth Dimension*, 191.
17   Desmond, *Being and the Between,* 501.
18   Armstrong, *The Great Transformation*, 317.
19   Desmond, *Being and the Between*, 184.
20   Penrose, *The Emperor's New Mind*, 554.
21   Jowett, *Plato: The Republic*, Book VI, 173.
22   Hick, *The Fifth Dimension*, 53.
23   Brann, Kalkavage, Salem, *Plato's Phaedo*, 109 E.
24   Ibid.
25   Jowett, *Plato: The Republic*, Book X, 273.
26   Jowett, *Plato: The Republic*, Book VI, 178,179.
27   Ibid, 178.
28   Ibid, 179.
29   Brann, Kalkavage, Salem, *Plato's Phaedo*, 106 E, 89.
30   Ibid, 105 E, 88.
31   Ibid, 105 A, 87.
32   Ibid, 105 B, 87.
33   Tolle, *A New Earth*, 128.
34   Brann, Kalkavage, Salem, *Plato's Phaedo*, 107 C, 90.
35   Cress, *Rene Descartes; Meditations on First Philosophy*, Synopsis, 54.
36   Cress, *Rene Descartes; Meditations on First Philosophy*, Synopsis, 55.

37   Ibid, Meditations One, 60.
38   Ibid, Meditation Two, 65.
39   Ibid, Meditation Two, 65.
40   Ibid, Meditation Three, 78.
41   Ibid, Meditation Three, 75.
42   Ibid, Meditation, Six, 98.
43   Ibid, Meditation Six, 98.
44   Ibid, Synopsis, 55.

Chapter Five

1   Jung; On Life After Death in Yates; *Jung on Death and Immortality*, 139.
2   Greene, *The Elegant Universe*, 104.
3   Heisenberg, *Physics and Humanism*, 88.
4   Heisenberg, *Physics and Humanism*, 107.
5   Telang, *The Anugita; The Bhagavadagita*, 335.
6   Panda, *The Vibrating Universe*, 299, 302.
7   Greene, *The Elegant Universe*, 203.
8   Greene, *The Elegant Universe*, 378.
9   Panda, *The Vibrating Universe*, 391.
10   Ibid, 391.
11   Grey, *Return From Death*, 51.
12   Ring, *Heading Towards Omega*, 66.
13   Fenwick, Fenwick, *The Truth in the Light*, 69.
14   Fenwick, Fenwick, *The Truth in the Light*, 74.
15   Moody, *Reflections on Life after Life*, 18.
16   Greene, *The Elegant Universe*, 332.
17   Grey, *Return From Death*, 43.
18   Grey, *Return From Death*, 42.
19   Greene, *The Fabric of the Cosmos*, 114.
20   Greene, *The Fabric of the Cosmos*, 115.
21   Ibid, 116.
22   Ibid.
23   Grey, *Return From Death*, 46.
24   Ibid, 51.
25   Ibid, 31, 48.
26   Moody, *Life After Life*, 60.
27   Moody, *Life After Life*, 60.
28   Greene, *The Fabric of the Cosmos*, 442-443.

29 New Scientist, *Speed Boost Helps Quantum Codes on their way*, issue 2566, August 26, 2006.

30 Van Lommel, *Near-Death Experience, Consciousness, and the Brain*, World Futures, Vol. 62, 140.

31 Greene, *The Fabric of the Cosmos*, 51.

32 Fenwick, Fenwick, *The Truth in the Light*, 74.

33 Fenwick, Fenwick, *The Truth in the Light*, 74.

34 Penrose, *The Emperor's New Mind*, 554.

35 Stewart, C. Clarke, etc., *The Colours of Infinity*, 152.

36 Stewart, etc. *The Colours of Infinity*, 163.

37 Penrose, *The Emperor's New Mind*, 124-125.

38 Stewart, etc. *The Colours of Infinity*, 151.

39 Stewart, *The Colours of Infinity*, 160.

40 Greene, *The Fabric of the Cosmos*, 43.

41 Greene, *The Fabric of the Cosmos*, 76.

42 Ibid, 269-270.

43 Ibid, 482.

44 Barbour, *The End of Time*, 254.

45 Greene, *The Elegant Universe*, 379.

46 Hameroff, *More Neural Than Thou*, Towards a Science of Consciousness II, MIT Press, Cambridge, 1998.

47 Hameroff, *More Neural Than Thou*, Towards a Science of Consciousness II, MIT Press, Cambridge, 1998.

48 Hameroff, Neimark, *Morality at the Planck Scale*, Metanexus; www.metanexus.com.

49 Hameroff, *More Neural Than Thou*, Towards a Science of Consciousness II, MIT Press, Cambridge, 1998.

50 Panda, *The Vibrating Universe*, 337.

51 Hameroff, Neimark, *Morality at Planck Scale*, Metanexus; www.metanexus.net.

52 Van Lommel, *Near-Death Experience, Consciousness, and the Brain*, World Futures, Vol. 62, 146.

53 Ring, Valarino, *Lessons From the Light*, 187.

54 Van Lommel, *Near-Death Experience, Consciousness, and the Brain*, World Futures, Vol. 62, 146.

55 Phipps, Interview with Bruce Greyson, 05.09.16, www.wie.org/reincarnation.

56 Van Lommel, *Interview*, IANDS Conference, October 28, 2006

57 Tiller, *Lecture at McGill University*, November 29, 2005

58 Greene, *The Fabric of the Cosmos*, 50.

Chapter Six

1   The Holy Bible, *New Catholic Version*, Exodus, 3:14.
2   The Holy Bible, *New Catholic Version*, Exodus, 3:14, footnote.
3   Strobel, *The Case For A Creator*, 219, 225.
4   Panda, *The Vibrating Universe*, 345.
5   Strobel, *The Case For A Creator*, 263.
6   Hunt, *Infinite Mind*, 83.
7   Hunt, *Infinite Mind*, 84.
8   Ibid, 85.
9   Ibid, 85-86.
10   Ibid, 87.
11   Varela, *Sleeping, Dreaming, and Dying*, 194.
12   Neimark, *New Life for Near-Death*, Spirituality&Health, September/ October 2003.
13   Hameroff in *Consciousness*, Alsbury Film 2003.
14   Ring, *Heading Towards Omega*, 66.
15   Hamilton, *Scientific Proof of the Existence of God*, What Is Enlightenment? magazine, Vol. 11, Spring/summer 1997.
16   Newman in *Consciousness*, Alsbury Films, 2003.
17   Krell, *Basic Writings of Martin Heidegger*, 243.
18   Krell, *Basic Writings of Martin Heidegger*, 227-228.
19   Pagels, *The Gnostic Gospels*, 126, 125.
20   Cress, *Rene Descartes; Meditations on First Philosophy*, Meditation One, 60.
21   Cress, *Rene Descartes; Meditations on First Philosophy*, Meditation Three, 75.
22   Yates, *Jung on Death and Immortality*, 76.
23   Ibid, 76.
24   Bauman, *Post-modernity and its Discontents*, 26.
25   Pagels, *The Gnostic Gospels*, 124.
26   Bauman, *Post-modernity and its Discontents*, 26.
27   Bauman, *Post-modernity and its Discontents*, 27.
28   Nyima Rinpoche, *The Bardo Guidebook*, 139.
29   Fenwick, Fenwick, *The Truth in the Light*, 57.
30   Nyima Rinpoche, *The Bardo Guidebook*, 137, 131.

Chapter Seven

1   Bauman, *Mortality, Immortality and Other Life Strategies*, Cambridge; Polity Press, 1992.

2   Benedict, *Reason, Religion, and God's Will*, Insight; The Gazette, September 24, 2006.
3   Harting, *Death Concerns Us All*, Helse Magazine, January, 2005.
4   Johansen, *The European History of Philosophy*, 547.
5   Sachs, *Perfect Endings*, 9.
6   Fenwick, Fenwick, *The Truth in the Light*, 120.
7   Sachs, *Perfect Endings*, 8-9.
8   Sachs, *Perfect Endings*, 10.
9   Fenwick, Fenwick, *The Truth in the Light*, 68.
10 Fenwick, Fenwick, *The Truth in the Light*, 72-73.
11 Ibid, 70.
12 Ibid, 71-72.
13 Ibid, 70-71.
14 Piper, *90 Minutes in Heaven*, 33.
15 Norbu, *The Small Golden Key*, 99.
16 Norbu, *The Small Golden Key*, 99-100.
17 Thurman, *The Tibetan Book of the Dead*, 42.
18 Soygal Rinpoche, *The Tibetan Book of Living and Dying*, 248.
19 Moody, *Life After Life*, 37.
20 Fenwick, Fenwick, *The Truth in the Light*, 10.
21 Norbu, *The Small Golden Key*, 100.
22 Nyima Rinpoche, *The Bardo Guidebook*, 112.
23 Nyima Rinpoche, *The Bardo Guidebook*, 114.
24 Soygal Rinpoche, *The Tibetan Book of Living and Dying*, 263.
25 Nyima Rinpoche, *The Bardo Guidebook*, 117.
26 Nyima Rinpoche, *The Bardo Guidebook*, 14-15.
27 Grey, *Return From Death*, 31.
28 Fenwick, Fenwick, *The Truth in the Light*, 74.
29 Grey, *Return From Death*, 31.
30 Nyima, *The Bardo Guidebook*, 15.
31 Fenwick, Fenwick, *The Truth in the Light*, 69.
32 Fenwick, Fenwick, *The Truth in the Light*, 69.
33 Ibid, 12.
34 Ibid, 74.
35 Ibid, 115.
36 Jung, Letters, Vol. 1, 343 in Yates, *Jung on Death and Immortality*, 6.
37 Brann, Kalkavage, Salem, *Plato's Phaedo*, 110 B, 93.
38 Ibid, 111 B, 94.
39 Moody, *Life After Life*, 97.
40 Fenwick, Fenwick, *The Truth in the Light*, 69.
41 Fenwick, Fenwick, *The Truth in the Light*, 58.

42   Ibid, 72.
43   Ibid, 168.
44   Ring, Valarino, *Lessons From the Light*, 43.

Chapter Eight

1   Helminski, *Rumi Daylight*, 160.
2   Moody, *Life After Life*, 60.
3   Phipps, *Death, Rebirth, and Everything in Between*, What Is Enlightenment? Vol. 32, March-May 2006, 79.
4   Brinkley, *Saved by the Light*, 17.
5   Moody, *Life After Life*, 65.
6   Moody, *Reflections on Life After Life*, 37.
7   Grey, *Return From Death*, 58.
8   Fenwick, Fenwick, *The Truth in the Light*, 188.
9   Atwater, *The Complete Idiot's Guide to Near-Death Experiences*, 30.
10   Greene, Krippne, Panoramic Vision, in Doore, *What Survives?* 65.
11   Long, *Near Death Experience*, www.nderf.org, overview.
12   Fenwick, Fenwick, *The Truth in the Light*, 191.
13   Fenwick, Fenwick, *The Truth in the Light*, 115.
14   Ibid, 120.
15   Grey, *Return From Death*, 56.
16   Latham, Howlett, *Dictionary of Medieval Latin from British Sources*, Volume I.
17   Liddell, Scott, *A Greek-English Lexicon*, Volume I.
18   Evans-Wentz, *The Tibetan Book of the dead*, 37.
19   Jung, *Man and His Symbols*, 218.
20   Sogyal Rinpoche, *The Tibetan Book of Living and Dying*, 259.
21   Brinkley, *Saved by the Light*, 25.
22   Varela, *Sleeping, Dreaming, and Dying*, 185.
23   Moody, *Life After Life*, 61-62.
24   Fenwick, *The Truth in the Light*, 69, 191.
25   Moody, *Reflections on Life after Life*, 36.
26   Revel, Ricard, *The Monk and the Philosopher*, 238.
27   *What Is Enlightenment?* Magazine, Vol. 32, March-May, 2006, 79.
28   Liddell and Scott, *A Greek-English Lexicon*, 77.
29   Ibid.
30   Liddell and Scott, *A Greek-English Lexicon*, 77.
31   Ibid.
32   Pagels, *The Gnostic Gospels*, 125.

33   Ibid. 124.
34   Moody, *Life After Life*, 98.
35   Dyer, *There is a Spiritual Solution to Every Problem*, 97-98.
36   Yusuf Ali, *The Holy Quran*, Surah 98:6.
37   Thurman, *The Tibetan Book of the Dead*, 130.
38   Hunt, *Infinite Mind*, 88.
39   Kierkegaard, *The Concept of Angst*, § 3 – 5.
40   Revel, Ricard, *The Monk and the Philosopher*, 238.
41   Jastrow, *A Dictionary of the Targumim, The Talmud Babli*, 1506.
42   Varela, *Sleeping, Dreaming and Dying*, 196.
43   Moody, *Reflections on Life after Life*, 38.
44   Soygal Rinpoche, *The Tibetan Book of Living and Dying*, 292.
45   Grey, *Return From Death*, 67.
46   Fenwick, Fenwick, *The Truth in the Light*, 190.
47   Knoblauch, Schmied, Schnettler, *Different kinds of Near-Death Experience,* Journal of Near-Death Studies, Vol. 20 #1, 2001, 25.
48   Morse, *Transformed by the Light*, 121.
49   Grey, *Return From Death*, 191.
50   Moody, *Life After Life*, 61-62.
51   Moody, *Life After Life*, 64.
52   Fenwick, Fenwick, *The Truth in the Light*, 114.
53   Yates, *Jung on Death and Immortality*, 7.
54   Yates, *Jung on Death and Immortality*, 8.
55   Jung; Psychology of the Transference in Yates; *Jung on Death and Immortality*, 74.
56   Jung; Psychology of the Transference in Yates; *Jung on Death and Immortality*, 75.
57   The Barna Group, *Americans Are Most Likely to Base Truth on Feelings*, February 12, 2002, www.barna.org.
58   The Barna Group, *Americans Are Most Likely to Base Truth on Feelings*, February 12, 2002, www.barna.org.
59   Abernathy, Exploring Religious America, Religion&Ethics Newsweekly, April 26, 2002.
60   The Barna Group, *Americans Are Most Likely to Base Truth on Feelings*, February 12, 2002, www.barna.org.
61   Holy Bible, NT, Matthew 5:30.
62   Axiom, *The Dhammapada*, 44.
63   Grey, *Return From Death*, 68.
64   Brinkley, *Saved by the Light*, 22-23.
65   Brinkley, *Saved by the Light*, 23-24.
66   Fenwick, Fenwick, *The Truth in the Light*, 114.

[67]   Robinson, The Gospel of Mary; *The Nag Hammadi Library*, 525.
[68]   Jowett, *Plato: The Republic*, 274.
[69]   Dyer, *There is a Spiritual Solution to Every Problem*, 97-98.
[70]   Fenwick, Fenwick, *The Truth in the Light*, 263.
[71]   Dalai Lama, *Ethics for the New Millennium*, 168-169.
[72]   Ibid. 288.
[73]   Holy Bible, NT, Matthew 25:42.
[74]   Cohen, *Jacques Derrida and the Humanities*, 35.
[75]   Lampe, *A Patristic Greek Lexicon*, 31.
[76]   Grey, *Return From Death*, 71.
[77]   Lampe, *A Patristic Greek Lexicon*, 1375.
[78]   Moody, *Reflections on Life after Life*, 26-27.
[79]   Ibid. 28.
[80]   Soygal Rinpoche, *The Tibetan Book of Living and Dying*, 14.
[81]   Doore, *What Survives?* 247.
[82]   Varela, *Sleeping, Dreaming, and Dying*, 185.
[83]   Brinkley, *Saved by the Light*, 18.

Chapter Nine

[1]   The Great Law of Peace
[2]   Leviticus 19:18.
[3]   The Bible, Matthew 7:12.
[4]   Fourth Hadith of an-Nawawi 13.
[5]   Confucianism, Analects 15:23.
[6]   Mahabharata 5.1517.
[7]   Samyutta Nikaya 353.
[8]   Merriam-Webster's Collegiate Dictionary, 973.
[9]   Ring, Valarino, *Lessons From the Light*, 176.
[10]   Ring, Valarino, *Lessons From the Light*, 177.
[11]   Ring, Valarino, *Lessons From the Light*, Foreword xviii.
[12]   Phipps, Interview with Bruce Greyson, 05.09.16, www.wie.org/reincarnation.
[13]   Wilson, *From So Simple A Beginning*, 837.
[14]   Penrose, *The Emperor's New Mind*, 556.
[15]   Giberson, *The Man Who Fell to Earth*, Science & Spirit; www.science-spirit.org.
[16]   Armstrong, *The Great Transformation*, 381.
[17]   *Exploring Religious America*, Religion & Newsweekly, April 26, 2002.

[18]   Armstrong, *The Great Transformation*, 391.
[19]   Fenwick, Fenwick, *The Truth in the Light*, 12.
[20]   Fenwick, Fenwick, *The Truth in the Light*, 69.
[21]   Atwater, *The Complete Idiot's Guide to Near-Death Experiences*, 141.
[22]   Atwater, *The Complete Idiot's Guide to Near-Death Experiences*, 391
[23]   Ring, *Heading Towards Omega*, 255.
[24]   Grey, *Return From Death*, 193.
[25]   Soygal Rinpoche, *The Tibetan Book of Living and Dying*, 332.
[26]   Holy Bible, *New Testament*, 1 John, 4:16.
[27]   Holy Bible, *New Testament*, 1 John, 4:11.
[28]   Carroll, *Constantine's Sword*, 353.
[29]   Ring, Valarino, *Lessons From the Light*, 187.
[30]   Ring, Valarino, *Lessons From the Light*, 187.
[31]   Ring, Valarino, *Lessons From the Light*, foreword, xii.
[32]   Neimark, *New Life for Near-Death*, Spirituality & Health, Sept/Oct. issue 2003.
[33]   Ring, Valarino, *Lessons from the Light*, foreword, xix.
[34]   Moody, *Life After Life*, 65.
[35]   Mumford, *Celebrating Death*, 137.
[36]   Grey, *Return From Death*, 194.
[37]   Ring, Valarino, *Lessons from the Light*, foreword xviii.
[38]   Fenwick, Fenwick, *The Truth in the Light*, 185.
[39]   Ring, *Headed Towards Omega*, 317.
[40]   Ibid, 301.
[41]   Ibid, 302.
[42]   Ibid, 303.
[43]   Ibid, 301.
[44]   Ibid, 317.
[45]   Atwater, *The Complete Idiot's Guide to Near-Death Experiences*, 176.
[46]   Greyson, E-mail exchange, November 9, 2006.
[47]   Ring, *Heading Towards Omega*, 143.
[48]   The Bible, *New Testament*, 1 John, 3:18-20.
[49]   The Bible, *New Testament*, 1 John, 4:16.
[50]   Armstrong, *The Great Transformation*, 317.
[51]   Pagels, *Beyond Belief*, Back cover.
[52]   Ring, Valarino, *Lessons From the Light*, 193.
[53]   Yogananda, *Autobiography of a Yogi*, 219, 271.
[54]   Greene, *The Elegant Universe*, 124.
[55]   Varela, *Sleeping, Dreaming, and Dying*, 194.
[56]   Liddell, Scott, *A Greek-English Lexicon*, 1115 / Lampe, *A Patristic Greek Lexicon*, 855.

57   Ring, Valarino, *Lessons From the Light*, 188.
58   Holy Bible, NT, 2 Corinthians 5:19
59   Holy Bible, NT, Math. 18:18
60   Desmond, *Being and the Between*, 531.
61   The Devotions of Rabi´a Adawiya, 51 in Sells, *Early Islamic Mysticism*.
62   Desmond, *Being and the Between*, 464.
63   Desmond, *Being and the Between*, 465/466.
64   Ibid, 468.
65   Liddell, Scott, *A Greek-English Lexicon*, 60.
66   Liddell, Scott, *A Greek-English Lexicon*, 1539.

Chapter Ten

1   Fenwick, Fenwick, *The Truth in the Light*, 81.
2   Carrol, *Constantine's Sword*, 316.
3   The Bible, *New Testament*, John 14:6
4   Time/CNN Poll, Gibbs, *Apocalypse Now*, Time, June 23, 2002.
5   Walters, *Heaven: Where is it? And how do we get there?* ABC, 2005.
6   Blitzer, *The Situation Room*, CNN, November 2, 2006.
7   Pagels, *Beyond Belief*, 147.
8   Sellers, *The Cave*, World Religions After 911, September 14, 2006.
9   Sellers, *The Cave*, World Religions After 911, September 14, 2006.
10   Ring, *Heading Towards Omega*, 162.
11   Said, *Culture and Imperialism*, 17.
12   Garrison, *America as Empire*, What is Enlightenment? Magazine, www.wie.org.
13   Annan, *Charlie Rose*, PBS, 13 December, 2006.
14   Perle in *America at a Crossroad*, PBS, April 16, 2007.
15   Farías, *Heidegger and Nazism*, 275-276.
16   Farías, *Heidegger and Nazism*, 276.
17   Bauman, *Post-modernity and its Discontents*, 29.
18   Douglas, *Purity and Danger*, 163.
19   Douglas, *Purity and Danger*, 163.
20   *Exploring Religious America*, Religion & Ethics Newsweekly, April 26, 2002.
21   Time/CNN Poll, Gibbs, *Apocalypse Now*, Time, June 23, 2002.
22   Dykman, *What we believe*, Time Magazine, October 30, 2006.
23   Douglas, *Purity and Danger*, 17-18.
24   Douglas, *Purity and Danger*, 17.

25 Lanza del Vasto, *The Chain of Violence*.
26 Poling, *Deliver Us From Evil*, Fortress Press, 1996.
27 Douglas, *Purity and Danger*, 178.
28 Fromm, *The Fear of Freedom*, 154.
29 Fromm, *The Fear of Freedom*, 155.
30 Helminski, *Women of Sufism*.
31 Huntington, *The Clash of Civilizations?*, in Foreign Affairs, Vol. 72 nu. 3, 1993.
32 Hardy, *The Middle Ground on Islam and West*, BBC News, 19 February, 2007.
33 America at a Crossroad, PBS, April 20, 2007.
34 Kristof, *Believe it, or not*, CNN.com, August 15, 2003.
35 CBS News, *Creationism Trumps Evolution*, November 22, 2004.
36 Bauman, *Post-modernity and its Discontents*, 19.
37 Ibid, 21-22.
38 Ibid, 29.
39 Hardy, *The Middle Ground on Islam and West*, BBC News, February 19, 2007.
40 Beauchemin, *Fundamental Principles*, The Gazette, December 9, 2006.
41 Holy Bible, *New Testament*, Luke 6:42.
42 Fromm, *The Fear of Freedom*, 207.
43 Bauman, *Post-modernity and its Discontents*, 33.
44 *The Universal Declaration of Human Rights*, 1948, Art. 1.
45 Fromm, *The Fear of Freedom*, v.
46 Hunt, *Infinite mind*, 94.
47 Thurman, *The Tibetan Book of the Dead*, 33.
48 Fromm, *The Fear of Freedom*, 29.
49 Panda, *The Vibrating Universe*, 383.
50 Strobel, *The Case for A Creator*, 128.
51 Armstrong, *The Great Transformation*, 397.
52 Carroll, *Constantine's Sword*, 323-324.
53 Kennedy, American University, Washington D.C., June 10, 1963.
54 Naft, *Tikkun Olam: Perfecting the World*, www.innerfrontiers.org
55 Dalia Lama, *Ethics for the New Millennium*, 169.
56 Bauman, *Post-modernity and its Discontents*, 27.
57 SIPRI Report 2004
58 Cooper, *Anderson Cooper 360*, CNN, April 26, 2007.
59 *Casualties in the Iraq war*, CBC News, February 5, 2007.
60 *U.N. Blames Darfur Deaths On Sudan Government*, CBS News, November 3, 2006.

61   Kennedy, Inaugural Address, Washington D.C., January 20, 1961.
62   Kennedy, Inaugural Address, Washington D.C., January 20, 1961.
63   The Economist, *The New Powers in Giving*, July 1 st, 2006.
64   Dalia Lama, *Ethics for the New Millennium*, 172-173.
65   Robinson, The Gospel of Thomas, *The Nag Hammadi Library*, 129.

Chapter Eleven

1   Telang, Anugita; *Bhagavadagita*, 335.
2   Fenwick, Fenwick, *The Truth in the Light*, 135.
3   Greyson, Flynn, *The Near-Death Experience: Problems, Prospects, Perspectives,* 193.
4   Piper, *90 Minutes in Heaven*, 33.
5   Ring, Valarino, *Lessons From the Light*, 287.
6   Ring, Valarino, *Lessons From the Light*, 290.
7   Fenwick, Fenwick, *The Truth in the Light*, 62.
8   Fenwick, Fenwick, *The Truth in the Light*, 58, 69.
9   Ibid, 84-85.
10   Greyson, Flynn, *The Near-Death Experience: Problems, Prospects, Perspectives,* 191.
11   Greyson, Flynn, *The Near-Death Experience: Problems, Prospects, Perspectives,* 179.
12   Yates; *Jung on Death and Immortality*, 74-75.
13   Alvarado, *What Is Enlightenment?* Vol. 32, March-May 2006, 82.
14   Jong, *Interview,* IANDS Conference, October 27, 2006.
15   Atwater, *The Complete Idiot's Guide to Near-Death Experiences*, 182.
16   Morse, *Transformed by the Light,* 119-120.
17   Fenwick, Fenwick, *The Truth in the Light*, 79.
18   Fenwick, Fenwick, *The Truth in the Light*, 62.
19   Van Lommel, *Interview,* IANDS Conference, October 28, 2006.
20   Ring, Valarino, *Lessons From the Light*, 285-286.
21   Moody, *Life After Life*, 37.
22   Doore, *What survives?* 247.
23   Sogyal Rinpoche, *The Tibetan Book of Living and Dying*, 259.
24   Thurman, *The Tibetan Book of the Dead*, 122.
25   Soygal Rinpoche, *The Tibetan Book of Living and Dying*, 245-246.
26   Mumford, *Celebrating Death*, 119.
27   Fenwick, Fenwick, *The Truth in the Light*, 110.
28   Yates; *Jung on Death and Immortality*, 77.
29   Grey, *Return From Death*, 191.

30 Grey, *Return From Death*, 195.
31 Yates; Jung on Death and Immortality, 76.
32 Soygal, *The Tibetan Book of Living and Dying*, 293.
33 *The Search For Heaven*, Grizzly Adams Productions, 2005.
34 Bush, *Distressing Western Near-Death Experiences,* IANDS Conference, October 25, 2006.
35 Nyima, *The Bardo Guidebook*, 54.
36 Nyima, *The Bardo Guidebook*, 156.
37 Ibid, 85, 86.
38 Sells, *Early Islamic Mysticism*, Dev. 51.
39 Moss, *The Dreamers Book of the Dead*, 185.
40 Grey, *Return From Death*, 31, 46.
41 Fenwick, Fenwick, *The Truth in the Light*, 58.
42 Moody, *Life After Life*, 42.
43 Ring, Valarino, *Lessons from the Light*, 94.
44 Nyima Rinpoche, *The Bardo Guidebook*, 124.
45 Fremantle, Trungpa, *The Tibetan Book of the Dead*, foreword xvi.
46 Nyima, *The Bardo Guidebook*, 156.
47 Evans-Wentz, *The Tibetan Book of the Dead*, 91.
48 Evans-Wentz, *The Tibetan Book of the Dead*, 91.
49 Fenwick, Fenwick, *The Truth in the Light*, 74.
50 Moody, *Reflections on Life After Life*, 18.
51 Nyima, *The Bardo Guidebook*, 143.
52 Soygal Rinpoche, *The Tibetan Book of Living and Dying*, 297.
53 Thurman, *The Tibetan Book of the Dead*, 180, 126.
54 Thurman, *The Tibetan Book of the Dead*, 251.
55 Moody, *Life After Life*, 58.
56 Nydahl, *Beyond Life and Death*, Buddhism Today, Spring/Summer 2006, 20.
57 Lodo, *Bardo Teachings*, 6, 7.
58 Fenwick, Fenwick, *The Truth in the Light*, 68, 69.
59 Fenwick, Fenwick, *The Truth in the Light*, 69.
60 Soygal, *The Tibetan Book of Living and Dying*, 261.
61 Moss, *The Dreamers Book of the Dead*, 237.
62 Rangdrol, *The Mirror of Mindfulness*, 48.
63 Nyima, *The Bardo Guidebook*, 131.
64 Mumford, *Celebrating Death*, 117.
65 Thurman, *The Tibetan Book of the Dead*, 126, 125.
66 Varela, *Sleeping, Dreaming, and Dying*, 125.
67 Yates, *Jung on Death and Immortality*, 78.
68 Moss, *The Dreamers Book of the Dead*, 236.

69 Fenwick, Fenwick, *The Truth in the Light*, 6.

70 Moody, *Reflections on Life after Life*, 20.

71 Moody, *Reflections on Life after Life*, 19.

72 Fenwick, Fenwick, *The Truth in the light*, 30.

73 Fenwick, Fenwick, *The Truth in the light*, 51.

74 Ring, Valarino, *Lessons From the Light*, 189.

75 Fenwick, Fenwick, *The Truth in the Light*, 6.

76 Ring, Valarino, *Lessons From the Light*, 188.

77 Fenwick, Fenwick, *The Truth in the Light*, 128.

78 Fenwick, Fenwick, *The Truth in the Light*, 135.

79 Ibid, 115.

80 Ring, Valarino, *Lessons from the Light*, 44.

81 Ring, Valarino, *Lessons from the Light*, 45.

82 Ibid, 46.

Bibliography on Books

Abdullah, Yusuf Ali. *The Holy Quran.* Hertfordshire: Wordsworth Editions, 2000.

Armstrong, Karen. *The Great Transformation: The Beginning of our Religious Traditions.* Toronto: Alfred A. Knopf, 2006.

Atwater, P. M. H. *The Complete Idiot's Guide to Near-Death Experiences.* Indianapolis: Alpha Books, 2000.

Axiom, (Publishing). *The Dharmmapada.* Rochester: Grange Books, 2002.

Barbour, Julian. *The End of Time: The Next Revolution in Physics.* New York: Oxford University Press, 2001.

Bauman, Zygmunt. *Post-modernity and its Discontents.* Cambridge: Polity Press, 1997.

Bauman, Zygmunt. *Mortality, Immortality and Other Life Strategies.* Cambridge; Polity Press, 1992.

Brann, Eva, Kalkavage, Peter, and Salem, Eric. *Plato's Phaedo.* Newburyport: The Focus Classical Library, 1998.

Brinkley, Dannion. *Saved by the Light.* New York: HarperPaperpacks, 1995.

Budge, E. A. Wallis. *The Egyptian Book of the Dead.* New York: Dover, 1967.

Carroll, James. *Constantine's Sword: The Church and the Jews.* New York: Mariner Books, 2002.

Churton, Tobias. *Gnostic Philosophy: From Ancient Persia to Modern Times*. Rochester: Inner Traditions, 2005.

Cress, Donald A.; Descartes, Rene. *Discourse of Method and Meditations on First Philosophy*. Indianapolis: Hackett Publishing Company, 1998.

Cohen, T. *Jacques Derrida and the Humanities*. Cambridge: Cambridge University Press, 2001.

Desmond, William. *Being and the Between*. Albany: State University of New York Press, 1995.

Doore, Gary. *What Survives? Contemporary Exploration of Life After Death*. Los Angeles: Jeremy P. Tarcher, 1990.

Douglas, Mary. *Purity and Danger: An analysis of the concepts of pollution and taboo*. New York: Routledge, 1996.

Dyer, Wayne W. *There is a Spiritual Solution to Every Problem*. New York: Quill, 2003.

Evens-Wentz, W. Y. *The Tibetan Book of the Dead*. Delhi: Winsome Books India, 2004.

Farias, Victor. *Heidegger and Nazism*. Philadelphia: Temple University Press, 1989.

Fenwick, Peter, and Fenwick, Elizabeth. *The Truth in the Light: An Investigation of Over 300 Near-Death Experiences*. New York: Berkley Books, 1997.

Fremantle, Francesca and Trungpa, Chogyam. *The Tibetan Book of the Dead: The Great Liberation Through Hearing in the Bardo*. Boston: Shambhala South Asia Editions, 2000.

Fromm, Erich. *The Fear of Freedom*. London: Routledge, 1997.

Greene, Brian. *The Elegant Universe: Superstrings, hidden dimensions, and the quest of the ultimate theory*. New York: W. W. Norton & Company, 2003.

Greene, Brian. *The Fabric of the Cosmos: Space, Time, and the Texture of Reality*. New York: Alfred A. Knopf, 2004.

Grey, Margot. *Return From Death: An Exploration of the Near-Death Experience*. London: Arkana, 1985.

Greyson, Bruce, and Flynn, Charles, P. *The Near-Death Experience: Problems, Prospects, Perspectives*. Illinois: Charles C. Thomas, 1984.

Grof, Stanislav. *Psychology of the Future: Lessons from Modern Consciousness Research*. Valby: Borgen, 2001.

Heisenberg, Werner. *Physics and Humanism*. Copenhagen: Gads Forlag, 1959.

Helminski, Camille Adams. *Rumi Daylight: A Daybook of Spiritual Guidance*. Boston: Shambhala South Asia Editions, 2000.

Helminski, Camille Adams. *Women of Sufism: A Hidden Treasure*. Boston: Shambhala, 2003.

Hick, John. *The Fifth Dimension: An Exploration of the Spiritual Realm*. Oxford: Oneworld Publications, 1999.

Holy Bible, *New Testament: New Internation Version*. UK: Hodder & Stoughton, 1983.

Holy Bible, The. *New Catholic Version*. U.S.A.: Memorial Bibles, 1961.

Hunt, Valerie. *Infinite Mind: Science of the Human Vibrations of Consciousness*. Malibu: Malibu Publishing Co., 1995.

Jastrow, Marcus. *A Dictionary: Of the Targumim, the Talmud Babli and Yerushalmi, and the Midrashic Literature*. (Vol. 1.) London: E. Shapiro, Vallentine & Co., 1926.

Johansen, Karsten Friis. *The European History of Philosophy: Antiquity*. Copenhagen: Nyt Nordisk Forlag Arnold Busck, 1998.

Jowett, Benjamin, *Plato: The Republic*. Mineola: Dover Publications, 2000.

Jung, Carl, G. *Man and his Symbols*. USA/Canada: Dell Publishing, 1968.

Kant, Immanuel. *Prolegomena*. Frederiksberg: Det Lille Forlag, 1994.

Krell, David Farrel. *Martin Heidegger Basic Writings*. London: Routledge, 2002.

Kierkegaard, Soren. *The Concept of Angst*. Copenhagen: Borgen, 1998.

Lama, Dalai. *Ethics for the new millennium*. Copenhagen: Aschehoug, 2000.

Lama, Lodo. *Bardo Teachings: The Way of Death and Rebirth*. New York: Snow Lion Publications, 1987.

Lampe, G. W. H. *A Patristic Greek Lexicon*. Oxford: At the Clarendon Press, 1961.

Latham, R. E., and Howlett, D. R. *Dictionary of Medieval Latin From British Sources: Volume 1*. England: Oxford University Press, 1975/1981.

Lewis, James, R. *The Death and Afterlife Book: The Encyclopedia of Death, Near Death, and Life After Death*. Detroit: Visible Ink Press, 2001.

Liddell, Henry George and Scott, Robert. *A Greek-English Lexicon: Volume 1+2*. London: Oxford; At the Clarendon Press, 1940.

Liddell, Henry George and Scott, Robert. *A Greek-English Lexicon*. London: Oxford; At the Clarendon Press, 1882.

Moody, Raymond. *Life After Life*. New York: Bantam Books, 1976.

Moody, Raymond. *Reflections on Life After Life*. Harrisburg: Stackpole Books, 1977.

Morse, Melvin, and Perry, Paul. *Transformed by the Light: The Powerful Effects of Near- Death Experiences on People's Lives*. New York: Villard Books, 1992.

Moss, Robert. *The Dreamers Book of the Dead: A Soul Traveler's Guide to Death, Dying, and the other side*. Rochester: Destiny Books, 2005.

Mumford, John. *Celebrating Death: Life after Death Beginning or End?* Dehli: New Age Books, 2004.

Norbu, Thinley. *The Small Golden Key: To the Treasure of the Various Essential Necessities of General and Extraordinary Buddhist Dharma*. Boston: Shambhala South Asia Edition, 1993.

Panda, N. C. *The Vibrating Universe*. Delhi: Motital Banarsidass Publishers, 1995/2000.

Pagels, Elaine. *Beyond Belief: The Secret Gospel of Thomas*. New York: Vintage Books, 2003.

Pagels, Elaine. *The Gnostic Gospels*. New York: Vintage Books, 1979.

Penrose, Roger. *The Emperor's New Mind*. Oxford: Oxford University Press, 1989.

Piper, Don, and Murphey, Cecil. *90 Minutes in Heaven: A True Story of Death and Life*. Michigan: Revell, 2004.

Rangdrol, Tsele Natsok. *The Mirror of Mindfulness: The Cycle of the Four Bardo's*. Delhi: Rupa, 2002.

Revel, Jean-Francois and Ricard, Matthieu. *The Monk and the Philosopher: East Meets West in a Father-Son Dialogue*. London: Thorson, 1998.

Ring, Kenneth. *Heading Toward Omega: In Search of the Meaning of the Near-Death Experience*. New York: Quill, 1984.

Ring, Kenneth, and Valarino, Evelyn Elsaesser. *Lessons From the Light: What we can learn from the near-death experience*. Needham: Moment Point Press, 2000.

Rinpoche, Soygal. *The Tibetan Book of Living and Dying*. London: Rider, 1998.

Rinpoche, Nyima, Chokyi. *The Bardo Guidebook*. Delhi: Rupa, 2003.

Robinson, James M. *The Nag Hammadi Library in English: The Definitive Translation of the Gnostic Scriptures*. San Francisco: Harper San Francisco, 1990.

Sachs, Robert. *Perfect Endings: A Conscious Approach to Dying and Death*. Rochester: Healing Arts Press, 1998.

Said, Edward W. *Culture and Imperialism*. London: Vintage. 1993.

Sells, Michael A. *Early Islamic Mysticism: Sufi, Quran, Maraj, Poetic and theological writings*. New York: Paulist Press.

Stewart, Ian, Clarke, Arthur C., etc. *The Colours of Infinity: The Beauty and Power of Fractals*. London: Clear books, 2006.

Strobel, Lee. *The Case for a Creator: A Journalist Investigates Scientific Evidence That Points Towards God*. Grand Rapids: Zondervan, 2004.

Telang, K. T. *The Bhagavadagita*. Delhi: Sri Satguru Publications, 2001.

Thurman, Robert A. F. *The Tibetan Book of the Dead*. New Delhi: Harper Collins, 2001.

Tolle, Eckhart. *A New Earth*. New York: Dutton, 2005.

Varela, Francisco J. *Sleeping, Dreaming, and Dying: An Exploration of Consciousness with the Dalai Lama*. Boston: Wisdom Publications, 1997.

Wilson, Edward O. *From So Simple a Beginning: The Four Great Books of Charles Darwin*. New York: Norton, 2006.

Yates, Jenny. *Jung on Death and Immortality*. Princeton: Princeton University Press, 1999.

Yogananda, Paramahansa. *Autobiography of a Yogi*. Bombay: Jaico Publishing House, 2001.

638755